THE CONCISE ATLAS OF
WINE

THE CONCISE ATLAS OF
WINE

Wina Born

Foreword by GEORGE H. REZEK, MD
Chairman North American Committee, International Wine and Food Society

CHARLES SCRIBNER'S SONS · NEW YORK

Copyright © Meijer Pers bv, Amsterdam, 1972

English language translation copyright © Ward Lock Limited, 1974

Copyright under the Berne Convention

First published in Great Britain in 1974 by Ward Lock Limited, London

Library of Congress Catalog Card Number 74-7890

ISBN 0-684-14065-9

maps
Otto van Eersel

design
Mart Kempers and Joop de Nijs

printed and bound in Spain by Heraclio Fournier SA, Vitoria

photographs

	page
Sem Presser	40, 76
Ed Suister	17, 67, 80
Zefa:	
H. Adam	105
F. Walther	86, 88, 98
W. H. Müller	100
K. Helbig	139
M.S.	129
E. Hummel	130
H. Meusel	140
Ung. Werbestudio	134
W. Hasenberg	149
P. Phillips	143
E. G. Carle	112, 147
V. Rihsé	118
Magnum/ABC Press:	
Bruno Barbey	74, 75
Cartier Bresson	93
Marc Riboud	8, 23, 35, 36, 54, 57, 61
Fred Mayer	108, 115
Han Born	12, 12, 13, 14, 15, 18, 21, 26, 45, 49, 56, 60, 63, 69, 78, 89, 91, 92, 96, 104, 108, 117, 121, 127

The quotation from the Odyssey on page 29 is from R. Lattimore's translation.

Contents

Foreword

When one writes an *Atlas of Wine* one accepts a very formidable task. To treat the subject thoroughly would be impossible or would require many, many volumes. Obviously, if the reader should become interested in the wines of any one area it would behoove him to read works that specialize in the wines of that particular area, but Wina Born covers the whole field extremely well in a small book that can serve as a reference book for all wine-lovers.

The wine world is expanding at a very rapid rate and no longer can one think of it as meaning only France, Germany, Italy, Spain and Portugal. The vineyards of California, for example, since Prohibition was repealed, have made great progress in the production of quality wines. The Finger Lakes area of New York State is also producing quality wines in increasing amounts. As long as the demand for wine grows there will be a growth in the number of areas trying to produce fine wines. In the United States vineyards are now being planted in Oregon, Washington, throughout the Middle West and along the Atlantic Seaboard. Many of these vineyards are financed or owned by wealthy conglomerates and have almost unlimited resources, so that some degree of success is practically insured. Since grapes will grow in almost any temperate climate, and some not so temperate, they can produce a wine of a sort. The vineyards of Australia, South America, South Africa and Northern Africa are also expanding to meet the demand and reap some of the profits. The expansion will continue until the market is saturated or until the consuming public loses its love for wine or for a particular type of wine. For example, Madeira was once the most popular of wines and today the demand is so small that it is classified by many enologists as a dying wine. Tastes in wines and fashions change.

The wines of the newer vineyards do not have the glamour of the great French wines, but they do have their connoisseurs who take great pleasure in talking about the wines and almost as much pleasure in drinking their wines. It is said that wine has inspired poets, helped diplomats in their efforts to civilize the world and aided musicians to compose, and this does not have to be one of the great French or German wines. It can be any wine. Unfortunately the newer vineyards try to imitate the great wines of France and Germany, when they should develop a personality of their own. Even the greatest of California Cabernet Sauvignon will never be a great French claret, but it can be a great California wine surpassed by none.

The author has covered the wines of the world in her atlas, and this book should be a welcome addition to every wine-lover's library.

George H. Rezek

What is wine?

What is wine? This is a question that can be answered in many ways according to one's character, temperament, or philosophy of life. The poetically inclined might say that wine is bottled sunshine, or that it is the dark heart's blood of Mother Earth. A mystic might say that wine is the solace God gave to man after the Flood, the smile that Heaven bestows each year upon a corruptible world. An epicurean may see in wine enchantment for eye, nose and tongue, a subtle and refined pleasure for body and spirit. For the more prosaic, wine is simply the fermented juice of grapes, consisting of water, alcohol and a few volatile and stable elements that determine taste, smell and colour. There is truth in all these answers, for wine is all this and a good deal besides.

In some countries the laws governing trades' descriptions lay down that only the fermented juice of freshly picked grapes may be called wine: the fermented juice of other fruits may not be sold as wine, still less concoctions of raisins, colouring matter and yeast, or worse.

Although our age has managed to solve many of the riddles of nature, the secret of wine has not yet been wholly fathomed, for it is linked to that of life itself. Wine is still a miracle, one worked by living yeast cells. These cells, aided by time, convert the sweet, frothing grape juice, which itself lacks any nobility of taste or smell, into wine. And wine at its best is an infinitely complicated work of art of glowing, living colour, an interplay of subtle fragrances and aromas with equally subtle tastes, hardly to be described in words. Since Pasteur the action of the micro-organisms responsible for the process of fermentation has been known and so too are the chemical changes involved. Wine can be analysed in laboratories to show how much it contains of water, ethylalcohol, tannic and other acids, aldehydes and esters, dextrines, minerals, glycerine, albuminoids and colouring material. But so far there has been no adequate explanation of the bouquet of wine, which is at once the most intimate and most transient of its aspects and only to be found in wines of quality that have had due time to mature.

Why is it that this bouquet develops in one wine only after years have elapsed and in another after a much shorter period? Why does the bouquet of a wine evolve during maturation in the bottle, but in the barrel in drinks distilled from wine, such as Armagnac and Cognac? And why does wine from one vineyard have a bouquet that suggests violets, while wine from exactly the same variety of grape from a vineyard a mile away brings raspberries to mind? And why does one Beaujolais smell of newly opened roses and another of overblown ones?

No one can give complete answers to such questions, but it is assumed that the bouquet ultimately originates in the deepest levels to which the roots of the vine can penetrate, the *sous-sol* as the French call it. The roots can go down more than thirty feet into the ground and it is they that pass on to the wine its most subtle, most intimate qualities, derived from stone, gravel or chalk, qualities that only poets can attempt to convey in words.

The maturation of wine too remains a mystery that cannot be wholly explained in biological terms. Wine is unique among the products of the earth in that it can be said and be seen to have two 'lives'. First a life as a grape on the vine. The grape develops in June after pollination, grows and ripens, and then is picked and 'dies' in the winepress. As soon as the yeast cells have done their work and the seething must is still, the wine enters on its second phase of life – and this shows some remarkable resemblances to the life of man. Wine too goes through a recalcitrant and often unmanageable youth; and just as in man, the more difficult the wine is at this stage, the better the mature result is likely to be. This first youth, often full of problems, but also of promise, is ended when the wine is transferred from the vat to the bottle. It now stands at the beginning of its mature life. How it develops in its maturity depends on the innate qualities it has derived from Nature and the nurture and handling it has received in the vat. Again the human parallel: the greater the natural potential of a wine, the longer it may take for all its qualities to develop.

No one can say for certain how long a wine will need for its full development. There are fast-maturing wines and slow ones. It often depends on the year of their vintage and on the winery in which they matured, particularly its temperature and humidity. There are wines that reach maturity with amazing speed and others that take so long that the most patient vintner is likely to give up hope. There are wines of which no one expects much in their early stages but which suddenly reveal themselves possessed of unsuspected qualities, and others that never fulfil their early promise and remain stuck at some stage in their development. There are wines that are at their best when young and others that are best left to age. It is this living, constantly surprising aspect of wine with its human analogy that makes it so profoundly exciting, a constant source of interest.

It is sometimes thought that these considerations apply only to great, and expensive, wines. Fortunately this is not so. It applies to all wines, whether humble or expensive, that remain themselves and have a character of their own. The only exceptions are the low-priced wines represented by the *vins de pays* (*du pays* when a particular district is referred to) of France and their equivalents elsewhere. Visitors from outside the wine-growing countries sometimes confuse these with what the French term *vins de la région*. These are made by small growers and peasants for their own use. The manner of their making is fairly primitive; nature takes its course and meticulous handling in cellars is not part of the process. They can be engaging wines. They are drunk from France to Greece – in any district where vines are grown – either in the grower's home or in small country inns that produce their own wine or buy it from neighbours. They are wines with the fresh, uncomplicated charm of the countryside. They taste marvellous with the dishes of their own region. They have their own forthright character and speak of the soil they grow in.

However, as they have not had the benefit of careful and scientific cellar management they cannot travel, or tolerate a change in climate. Any tourist who returns from his holiday with a few bottles of these anonymous wines may well be disappointed. In northerly latitudes they often decline and lose their charm.

Vins de pays are very simple wines from vineyards which because of their soil and their position cannot yield wines of quality, only quantity. They cannot therefore lay claim to a registered and protected name and they do not have to measure up to any criteria of quality. They are made in bulk, as quickly and economically as possible, matured in concrete tanks, are usually filtered or treated in some other way to render them drinkable with a minimum of delay, and they are freely blended with wines of other provenance to produce a desired colour, alcohol content and taste. The progress from grape to bottle is swift, the price low, and the names given such wines are often decidedly romantic.

These simple wines are not necessarily bad. They just lack the individual character that can make wine so exciting and absorbing. But they can be pleasing for anyone who demands nothing more than a simple wine for everyday use. Wine is always wine, however simple, and merits Brantome's words: 'Wine is like a doctor, sometimes it brings healing, sometimes relief but always solace'. And to this we might add 'and always a sunnier view of life'. Or, like the Psalmist we can say, 'Wine . . . maketh glad the heart of man.'

The beginning of all wine is the grape that hangs on the vine waiting for the picker. The vine is an ancient plant. Its ancestors grew in the primeval forests of the Secondary period, when the dinosaurs strode the earth. Fossilized leaves and seeds of vines of the Tertiary have been found in many places in Europe – Champagne, the banks of the Rhine, the hills of Tokay and in the Rumanian Carpathians. These must have come from the true *Vitis vinifera*, parent stock of all today's vines. The vine is distributed throughout the temperate zones of both the northern and the southern hemispheres, roughly between latitudes 30 and 50. Here and there the vine has crept beyond these frontiers, as in the German Ahr valley, which lies just north of latitude 50, and in Dutch Limburg, where in recent years it has been growing as it did in the Middle Ages.

Adaptation to particular climatic conditions, crossings and improvements have led to the hundreds of varieties of grapes from which wine can be produced today (not all grapes produce wine). Among them are such noble kinds as the Riesling, the Pinot Noir and the Chardonnay; there are also many humbler varieties, and hybrids, crosses of *Vitis vinifera* with certain wild vines – but wines from these cannot lay claim to protected names.

The great art lies in choosing for a wine area the vines that give the best wine in its particular conditions of soil and climate. A vine that produces wine of high quality in one region may yield something of much

Riesling grapes

Chardonnay grapes

Gamay grapes

smaller stature in a different soil and climate. Cabernet Sauvignon, for example, is the grape that gives the finest Médocs, but also the simple wines of Anjou. It can also happen that a fine grape variety will produce two totally different but equally good wines in two different regions: excellent white wines are made from the Pinot Gris in Alsace and Hungary, but they are not at all alike in character.

The grape to a very large extent determines the character of the wine, although climate and soil too have a considerable influence, not to mention those yeast cells which can vary from district to district and appear to have a still mysterious influence on the character of the wine.

In vineyards on the northern edge of the wine-producing zone, where there is always the likelihood of spring frosts, the preferred grape will be a variety that buds late (such as the Riesling) and therefore is less likely to be spoiled by the unusually cold days, or Ice Saints as they are called in some Continental countries, that sometimes come in early May. In these northerly wine-growing districts black grapes are not planted – except in the Ahr valley – as these need a warm September if they are to form their colour properly.

There are wines that are made from one particular type of grape – and must be so made if they are to enjoy the protection of their registered name – such as the red Burgundies from the Pinot Noir, German Moselles from the Riesling, Beaujolais from the Gamay and sherry from the

Pinot Noir grapes

Palomino. Most wines, however, are made from more than one kind of grape, mixed in proportions that may vary from year to year. For example, three types of black grapes go into the winepresses to make red Médocs: Cabernet Sauvignon, Malbec and Merlot; two kinds are generally used for Champagne: white Chardonnay and the black Pinot Noir; and for Chianti three: red Sangiovese and Canaiolo and white Trebbiano. Even more varieties go into the Rhône wines: thirteen as a rule for the Châteauneuf-du-Pape.

There are certain types of grapes that have a clearly defined character of their own which they pass on to the wine. You can easily recognize them from the wine, often simply by holding your nose over the glass. This is especially true of grapes with a markedly spicy aroma, such as the various muscats. There are both white and black muscat grapes, which were used for wine as long ago as Ancient Greece. The finest Muscatel is the dry Muscat d'Alsace. Usually, however, such wines are rather sweet and not of particularly high quality.

The Gewürztraminer is a grape easily recognizable from the characteristically rich, spicy taste of its wine. Anyone who has cultivated a good nose for wine will always recognize the wonderful bouquet of a Riesling which smells of blossom, no matter whether it is Riesling from the

Moselle or from Alsace, from the Rheingau, Austria or Hungary. The Riesling bouquet can still be detected faintly even in the Madeira Sercial, a dry, fragrant Madeira made from the descendants of Riesling vines introduced into the island in about 1750. Two hundred years of growing in volcanic tuff and lava in a subtropical climate has not been able to eradicate the characteristics of the Riesling grape, which had its origins by the cool banks of the Rhine.

Viticulturists have also experimented with crossing different varieties of vines. One of the best known and most successful of these hybrids is that of Riesling and Sylvaner, the work of Professor Müller of Switzerland. In Germany this new variety is named Müller-Thurgau after him. In Luxembourg, where this hybrid does particularly well and gives excellent wine, it is usually referred to as the Riesling x Sylvaner, or more briefly as the Rivaner. It has the nobility of the Riesling and is at the same time easy to grow, like the Sylvaner.

Many grapes, or at least cuttings from a parent vine, have made long journeys. The Crusaders had a particular penchant for bringing back seedlings as souvenirs of their Middle Eastern adventures. Thibault IV, Count of Champagne, took home from Cyprus the Chardonnay that lives on gloriously in every bottle of Champagne. According to legend it was Crusaders who returned to France with the Syrrah, a black grape that is used for the wines of the Côtes du Rhône. The name is said to be a

Sauvignon grapes with pourriture noble

corruption of Shiraz, the town in Persia that was already famed for its wine in the time of the poet Omar Khayyam.

There is a tradition that the grape used for the Tokay d'Alsace was taken to that region in the fifteenth century by Lazarus von Schwandi, a knight who had brought it back from Hungary. However, this story does not really fit the facts, for the Tokay d'Alsace is not a Hungarian variety of grape but an ancient French Pinot Gris that made the journey in the opposite direction and is today established in the Lake Balaton area, where it produces a fine wine called Szürkebarát, 'Grey Friar'. On the other hand the renowned and almost legendary *vin jaune* of the French Jura does have distant Hungarian lineage: the Savagnin grape from which it is made was in fact brought from Hungary by an adventurous knight. Grapes still travel today, especially to the people's democracies of eastern Europe and to North America, where since World War II the hitherto comparatively simple viticulture has been put on a modern, scientific basis and quality vines have been introduced from France and Germany.

The vine likes stony soil which retains warmth and allows moisture to drain away. Winter temperatures do not harm it, so long as frosts are not too severe – as they were in the disastrous winter of 1959 when many fine vineyards around Bordeaux were ruined. It does like a mild, moist spring, sun in June when the tender, fragrant blossom comes out (Marie Antoinette had perfume distilled from vine blossom); it likes a little rain, but not hailstorms, in August; a fine, warm September with just occasional showers, so that the grapes can form their juice; and a dry, sunny October, with light mists in the morning when the pickers come to gather the heavy bunches.

A warm June means plentiful blossom and pollination, and therefore a lot of grapes; a sunny August and September produces abundant sugar, resulting in robust wines with a good alcohol content. June makes the quantity, they say in France, and August the quality. In Germany, however, they prefer a rather cooler August and September, because too much sugar in the grapes makes a German wine heavy and unbalanced. Thus a good year from the point of view of French wines is often a rather difficult one for German wines – which are then short of acids and hard to keep in consequence. French wines stand or fall on their alcohol content, German on their acids.

The life of the wine grower, which we like to idealize as a sunny existence among green hills and in fragrant-smelling cellars, is in fact one of hard toil with one eye constantly on the weather. Night frosts in spring are a calamity. A whole year's vintage can be destroyed in a night if the young shoots are attacked by frost, yet the grower must go on tending the vineyard all through the year just the same. Rain in June is a disaster because then the pollen is washed out of the blossom. Summer storms with rain or hail are a catastrophe: the leaves become torn and can no longer

Tipping grapes into collecting tubs

form sugar for the grapes, which consequently come to nothing. A damp August brings on moulds and parasites. If there is too much rain in September the grapes absorb excessive water and the wine is too thin. Rain in October during the vintage removes yeast cells from the grape skins and fermentation does not get under way. But if all goes well and new wine is born in October, the grower may then share the opinion once expressed by Dante, that a man who makes wine preserves sunshine.

The making of wine

Wine was not discovered as the result of human ingenuity – as was the art of distilling – but was created, spontaneously and naturally, out of grape juice. It was simply a logical progression of cause and effect in which man at first had a purely passive, though grateful, part to play. Only in the course of many centuries has he learned to control this natural phenomenon to some extent and to guide it in a desired direction. Modern biochemistry has taught us how wine comes into being and we have some measure of control over the whole process of fermentation but we do not know all the secrets of wine: many questions remain which science cannot fully answer.

Each year new wine is born naturally in the recesses of dark cellars. Every grower accepts it as a gift, as he does the coming into bud of his vines each spring. In many regions it is still customary for the grower reverently to doff his hat when he stands before a vat of fermenting must.

Nonetheless, although Nature has the leading role in the annual drama of the wine, man also has a real part to play. In France they like to illustrate this by the following anecdote. One fine morning a wine grower was standing at the doorway of his cellar when the priest came by. Greetings were exchanged, and talk about the weather. The peasant grower, knowing that his pastor appreciated a glass in season, invited him into the cellar to taste his wine. Monsieur le Curé tasted, and, conscious of his vocation, said, 'Excellent wine, splendid. You should be grateful to the good Lord for making it for you.' 'Indeed I am,' answered the farmer, 'but I would not like to think what would have become of the wine if He had had to see to it Himself!'

When the grapes are ripe in September or October they are picked and taken by the cartful as quickly as possible to the cellars. There they are stripped from the stalks and crushed. If red wine is being made black grapes are tipped into vats to ferment, skins and all. There the dark purple pulp lies, smelling of summer and ripe fruit. Less than twenty-four hours later the first indication of new life can be discerned in the dark mass of grapes. A rather sharp, sour scent can be detected in the sweet smell of the grapes and this comes more and more to predominate.

Carrying tubs of grapes, Hermitage, Côtes du Rhône

Bubbles rise from the depths, grow larger and reflect the scanty light of the cellar in iridescent colours. They follow one another upwards, in steadily increasing numbers. A dirty-pink scum forms on the surface of the must and grows thicker. Its surface is continually broken as the bubbles spurt and spatter through it and sometimes froth splashes several feet above the vat. This is the almost violent fermentation that turns the must into wine. This tumultuous process is caused by tiny micro-organisms, belonging to the saccharomyces, first studied under the microscope by the Dutch scientist Anthonie van Leeuwenhoek; they are commonly referred to as yeast cells. These cells occur naturally in ripe grapes in the form of a thin, waxy layer, sometimes poetically called the 'bloom'. When the grapes are pressed and the yeast cells come into contact with the grape juice they attack the sugar it contains and convert it into alcohol and carbon dioxide. The latter escapes through the scum: this is why no one should bend over a vat of fermenting must for too long for he could be overcome by the gas.

This fermentation process can only proceed satisfactorily in a favourable temperature – which is somewhere about the average temperature experienced on fine October days in regions south of latitude 50. In unfavourable years, when October is cold and the outside temperature drops to below 20°C, fermentation does not get properly under way and undesirable bacteria normally controlled by the yeast cells are able to gain a footing. These sour the must and the result is not wine but vinegar. For this reason in France, Germany and Austria, where October can sometimes be unexpectedly cold, cellars sometimes have to be heated. As too high temperatures cause the fermentation to proceed too violently, producing wine that is unbalanced and difficult to keep, fermentation vats in southerly wine-growing regions often have to be cooled by conducting water over their external surfaces.

The fermentation process is very complicated. Besides ethyl alcohol, other types of alcohol are produced, albeit in small quantities, which combine with the acids of the grape juice. This is where aroma, bouquet and subtle nuances of taste have their beginning, developing further as the wine matures. How this bouquet actually comes into being is not known precisely, still less what bouquet really is. When the yeast cells have converted all the grape sugar into alcohol they die off and sink to the bottom of the vat or tank. The must has become wine and, given good management in the cellar or winery, will be successfully aged there.

The processes described above are broadly applicable to red wine. The red colour develops during fermentation of black grapes that have been bruised or partly pressed with their skins. These skins release not only colouring matter but also certain other substances, such as tannic acid. Tannin is responsible for the tartness that makes a new wine 'harsh', but also makes it possible for it to age. If a wine is not one of the first rank this mass of crushed grapes will be finally pressed after only a few days' fermentation. The pressed juice is then left to ferment until the yeast cells have died off. The moment at which the pressing is done depends on the kind of wine being made. Wines that have to be drunk young are pressed quite quickly, before very much tannin has been released from the skins. By this means the wine more quickly achieves a pleasant roundness. This is the case with Beaujolais, for example, which is pressed after just five or six days – and after only two or three days if it is to be marketed within a few months as Beaujolais de Primeur. Beaujolais never has the deep red colour of a claret and contains much less tannin. Being short of tannin it is soon pleasantly drinkable, but cannot age.

High-grade red wines, such as the great clarets of the Médoc, are often not pressed at all. The must with all the skins is left in the vats until fermentation has run its entire course, after about two weeks. The skins and other impurities float to the top, forming a layer known as the *chapeau* or cap. The young wine is then drawn off into barrels for its first maturation.

Wines with any claim to excellence have to spend two years in the barrel. During this process the wine is transferred a number of times to clean barrels; by this means any impurities it has deposited are left behind in the old barrels and at the same time the wine is 'aired'. After two years the wine will have lost its first harshness and there is little or no risk of secondary fermentation: the wine has come to rest. If it were to remain longer in the barrel it would acquire an unpleasant woody taste. Truly great wines then proceed to develop their potential in the bottle – the bouquet, the balance and subtlety, all the properties that make them what they are.

The humbler red wines are not drawn off into wooden barrels after pressing, but into large tanks of glazed concrete or stainless steel. They are left in these until they stop fermenting, then they are filtered and cooled for a time. This causes them to deposit all their impurities in a short space of time and means that they can be bottled quite soon after the vintage. Sometimes they are also pasteurized to prevent any hint of secondary fermentation. Wines treated in this way are not capable of further perfection, for the elements that nourish it – all those floating particles – have been unceremoniously removed. Only very unpretentious wines, of which little is asked, are produced in this briskly efficient manner, often for sale at extremely low prices.

A tastevin is used for sampling wine from the cask

WHITE WINE

White wine can be made from black as well as white grapes, although it is mostly the latter that are used. For white wine the grapes are pressed as soon as they come into the winery. The juice, an extremely light green in colour, is drawn off into barrels (for the very good wines) or tanks, and in the course of a few hours fermentation begins. It proceeds exactly as in red wines. In establishments where white wines of quality are made there are long rows of small barrels with open bungholes out of which there surges a grey froth. It bubbles thickly above the holes and flows in broad streams down the sides of the barrels. As soon as the fermentation is over the young wine is transferred to clean barrels or tanks. During the cold winter months the wine deposits most of its sediment. The cellarmaster awaits the critical first warm days of spring when any young wine, and certainly white, shows a strong tendency to unrest and to second fermentation. As soon as the wine is quiet again it is bottled. White wines mature for at most nine months in the barrel. After this it depends on the type of wine whether it is allowed to develop further in the bottle or whether it is drunk young.

ROSÉ WINES

Grapes that actually have pink flesh are very rare. Rosé wines are nearly always made from black grapes which are left to stand in their bruised state for a short time – sometimes no more than twelve hours, but usually twenty-four – until fermentation has just begun. The grapes are then pressed immediately. This means the must has absorbed just a little of the colouring matter from the grape skins, and no tannin. In this way rosé wine acquires the pink colour that gives it its name, but not the typical properties of a red wine. Like white wines, rosés are bottled young. With very few exceptions they are not wines of high quality and they improve little or not at all in the bottle. They are quickly made and not intended for keeping.

SWEET WINES

Grapes contain sugar. The more sun the leaves have absorbed, the more sugar the grapes are able to form. As alcohol is the result of the conversion of sugar, alcoholic strength will therefore depend on the original sweetness of the grapes. Wines from southerly regions, where the grapes are very sweet, are usually heavier than wines from further north; similarly wines from fine, sunny years have a greater alcoholic content than those from wet, chilly ones. During fermentation the yeast cells, as it were, do their best to convert all the sugar in the must into alcohol. In so doing they bring about their own destruction. They furiously produce alcohol, but the higher the alcohol content of the must becomes, the more difficult their existence: yeast cells cannot survive in surroundings of more than fifteen per cent alcohol. Usually all the sugar is used up before this critical limit is reached. Most wines therefore are 'dry', that is to say they contain no sugar surplus. If, however, a non-dry, i.e. a wine of some degree of

sweetness, is desired, special methods have to be employed. There are various possibilities.

1   Grapes with such a high sugar content are used that the fifteen per cent limit is reached before all the sugar has been converted and unfermented sugar remains in the wine. But in practice there are very few grapes that have this amount of sugar naturally. A higher concentration of sugar is easy to obtain: grapes are simply left to dry and shrivel, either on the vine or after picking. The water content evaporates, but the sugar is left behind. If these partly dried grapes are pressed, the must obtained has a very high concentration of sugar which cannot all be converted before the fifteen per cent limit has been achieved. The result is a sweet wine of high alcohol content. Such wines can be of exceptional quality. Examples are the famous golden wines from Sauternes, the costly *Trockenbeerenauslesen* from the Rheingau and the legendary Tokays of Hungary, all of which are made from grapes dried on the vine and are all affected by a particular rot or fungus that gives them their distinctive taste. There are also relatively humble wines in this category, such as the Malaga, which is made from grapes that have been picked and then spread on mats to dry in the sun.

2   The fermentation process can be interrupted before all the sugar has been converted. The most effective way of doing this is to add pure wine alcohol when fermentation is halfway to completion so that the fifteen per cent limit is attained and the yeast cells die before all the sugar has been converted. This method is applied to port, for example, (*see* Fortified Wines), and also to Samos and, in its most extreme form, to certain other Greek and Spanish white wines. In these the must is scarcely allowed to start to ferment and the alcohol is added when all the sugar is still present; the results of this method can scarcely be termed wine. Wine with just a small amount of sugar can be obtained by arresting fermentation at a point when most of the sugar has been used up. There are three methods: refrigerating the must so that the yeast cells can no longer act; adding sulphur; and pasteurization, which kills the yeast cells. These methods,

however, are never applied to wines of any quality, for they would do violence to their character. They are customary for cheap white wines that are largely sold on the measure of sweetness so obtained. As there is a tendency towards further fermentation if yeast cells have been merely rendered inactive by the addition of sulphur or by refrigeration, such wines have to be pasteurized or treated with sulphur again when they are bottled.

FORTIFIED WINES

It is not known for certain where people first had the idea of pouring wine into a distilling vessel, heating it until the alcohol vapour escaped, and then catching this vapour and cooling it to obtain pure alcohol. The Arabs are usually given the credit, although there are indications that the Greeks had discovered the art centuries before them. But it was Arab alchemists in the early Middle Ages in Spain who perfected the art and found a practical application for it. And this is why the spirit released in the vessel, and the old type of distilling apparatus itself, are still known by their Arabic names of alcohol and alembic. In Spain these alchemists had abundant wine available for their experiments. Once they had learned to extract the fiery spirit of the wine in this way they proceeded with their experiments and mixed wine with pure alcohol. If they were good Muslims they could not drink the results themselves, but they used these fortified wines in their chemical and medical researches. Thus it is thanks to Arab alchemists that we can drink apéritif wines, such as port, sherry, Madeira, vermouth, all of which consist of wine with added alcohol. This of course gives them a higher alcoholic content than wine could ever attain naturally. Alcohol is added to sherry when the fermentation is complete and the wine therefore no longer contains sugar; this is what gives sherry its dry character. For medium or sweet sherry a certain amount of sweet wine has to be added. In making port, however, and some types of Madeira too, the alcohol is added during the fermentation process. The alcoholic content becomes so high that the yeast cells are killed off and unfermented sugar remains in the wine. Port is therefore a rather sweet wine with a high alcohol content. Most fortified wines must stay appreciably longer in the vat than normal wines to achieve their maturity.

SPARKLING WINES

The pleasant tingling sensation that some wines produce on the tongue is caused by tiny bubbles of carbon dioxide released immediately the bottle is uncorked. These bubbles can occur in the wine in various ways.

1   Entirely naturally, through secondary fermentation in the bottle. In a cool climate in which Octobers can be quite chilly the wine does not always have the chance of complete fermentation: yeast cells cease to be active if it becomes too cold. This means that living yeast cells and a small residue of unfermented sugar are left in the wine. When the first warm days

come in the following spring these yeast cells become active again and quickly complete the process of converting that residue of sugar into alcohol. Wines from chalky soil possess this tendency to secondary fermentation most strongly. In this second fermentation, which is far less tumultuous than the first process, carbon dioxide is produced once more. If the wine is in the barrel by this time, then the carbon dioxide can escape through the bunghole and after a few weeks the wine settles down again. To ascertain whether fermentation is finally over so that he can transfer the wine to a new barrel, the cellarmaster listens to the wine with his ear against the barrel. If on the other hand the wine is bottled before secondary fermentation is complete, and securely corked so that the carbon dioxide cannot escape, then the gas remains in solution in the wine until the bottle is uncorked and the wine is poured foaming into the glass. This is the best and the most natural method of making sparkling wine, but also the most costly. Moreover, by no means all wines are suitable for it. As the method was perfected in Champagne in the seventeenth century (and the wines of Champagne, from a cool climate and grown on chalky soil, were particularly suitable) this is termed the *méthode champenoise.*

Sparkling wines from districts other than Champagne which are made by this natural method are entitled to carry the words *méthode champenoise* on their labels, but not the name Champagne. This is reserved exclusively for sparkling wines from Champagne itself. Further details are given in the section devoted to Champagne.

2   A less expensive method is to let the wine undergo its secondary fermentation not in bottles but in pressurized tanks, after which it is bottled. This method is not as a rule used for first-class wines and the secondary fermentation is not left to depend on the natural properties of the wine, but is induced by the addition of sugar and yeast cultures. This method is much used for cheap German Sekt.

3   The cheapest method of all is simply pumping in the carbon dioxide. This is used widely for the so-called *Perlweine* of Germany and for slightly sparkling small rosés. The difference between the results of this process and the natural method is immediately apparent: injected carbon dioxide gives larger bubbles which disappear more quickly.

There are also sparkling wines, such as some from the Loire and from the south of France, which are the result of a slight secondary fermentation in the bottle. This phenomenon can also be observed in Moselles. In Germany the adjective *spritzig* describes the resulting wine. Strictly speaking it is due to a fault in the wine – it often occurs when the wine is bottled too early or fermentation is not properly controlled. There is sometimes a greater tendency to secondary fermentation in some years than others – but the fault can be an attractive one and it is sometimes produced deliberately, although never in high-class wines.

*Mosaic on Cyprus showing Dionysus,
Greek god of wine*

The story of wine

The word wine is of ancient lineage. Some have even sought to derive it from the Sanskrit *vena*, 'that which is poured out'. There are obviously related words in a number of the Indo-European languages for this drink of fermented grape juice that has had the power to take men out of themselves and to gladden their hearts. In Caucasian languages the word became *gvine* or *ghini*, in Greek *oinos* and in Latin *vinum*. As the vine spread to the barbarian north, the Latin name travelled with it, to Gaul where it eventually became the French *vin*, and to the Germanic tribesmen on the Rhine who adapted it to their pronunciation so that ultimately it developed into English wine, Dutch *wijn* and German *Wein*. The Celts too acquired the word: in Welsh it is *gwin* and in Gaelic *fion*.

But all the stories, all the myths point in the direction of Persia, the region south of the Caucasus. According to the Bible, Noah was the first man to grow vines and the first to get drunk. Remarkably enough, wild vines closely akin to the cultivated kind still grow in the area around Mount Ararat, where in the Bible story Noah's ark came to rest after the Flood.

In Greek mythology the wine god Dionysus brought the vine to Greece from Asia Minor. And one of the oldest stories about the origin of wine comes from Persia. King Dsemsit was so fond of grapes that he stored them in stone pitchers in his cellar for when they were out of season. However, slaves working in this enclosed cellar were overcome (by carbon dioxide given off by the fermenting grapes) and it was thought that the grapes had become poisonous. A rejected favourite, wanting to do away with herself, drank some of the dark, fragrant liquid and came singing and dancing, shining-eyed, out of the cellar, to the considerable amazement of the king. The radiant and happy creature was restored to favour and Dsemsit now knew how he could enliven his future feasts: with grape juice kept in jars in the cellar for half a year, there to turn in some mysterious way into a miraculous drink with the power of making an unhappy soul happy.

Not only ancient myths but also archaeology points to Persia. The earliest traces of viticulture so far discovered have been found in Neolithic settlements in Iran. Wine was first mentioned in a written source about 3000 BC, in clay tablets found in ancient Ur of the Chaldees, the capital of

Sumeria, and in Egyptian hieroglyphics. Unlike most of the peoples of the ancient world the Sumerians had a wine goddess, not a wine god. She was Gestin, one of the many manifestations of the ancient fertility goddess, the Earth Mother. In the Babylonian Gilgamesh epic too it was a woman who first made wine 'from the sinuous Tree of Life with its dark bunches'.

The Egyptian god Osiris was termed the 'Lord of the Wine and the Flood'. The Egyptians, who had probably got the vine from Syria or the land of the Hittites, practised viticulture with a good deal of skill and intelligence, as tomb paintings in the pyramids show. They trained the vines up on high trellises, which was very practical in a country with as much sun as Egypt, for it enabled the grapes to ripen in the shade and this prevented the wine from being too heavy. The grapes were trodden by foot but the forerunner of the modern horizontal winepress was already in use: the crushed grapes went into a sack suspended horizontally between two spindles. When these were turned in opposing directions the juice was squeezed from the grapes. The ancient Egyptians also had a system of naming and labelling their wines, for the stone jars found in many tomb chambers bear a seal with the hieroglyph of their vineyard and of the merchant.

The Phoenicians, the stout-hearted merchant seamen of the Mediterranean, carried wine in their swift, slender galleys from Lebanon and Syria to Egypt, Egyptian wine to Crete and the coasts of the Black Sea, Cypriot wine to the harbours of Phoenicia; by about 1500 BC there was already an extensive wine trade in existence. The prophet Hosea sang of the wine of Lebanon: '. . . they shall revive as the corn, and grow as the vine: the scent thereof shall be as the wine of Lebanon.' The beautiful Queen of Sheba and Solomon together drank wine from the legendary En-gedi in Cyprus. 'My beloved is unto me as a cluster of camphire in the vineyards of En-gedi' was one of the poetic comparisons she found in the Song of Songs.

Israel herself had fine vineyards; that they were admirably cared for is suggested by a Talmudic law which states that no war can be waged during the vintage. A picture of stirring events in these vineyards is conjured up by the story of the six hundred men of the tribe of Benjamin who survived a massacre of their people, including all the women and children, by the men of Israel. The Benjaminites, bereft of wives and offspring, took their revenge in picturesque fashion, as is related in the soberly effective language of the Authorized Version:

Behold, there is a feast of the Lord in Shiloh yearly. . . . Go and lie in wait in the vineyards; and see, and, behold, if the daughters of Shiloh come out to dance in dances, then come ye out of the vineyards, and catch you every man his wife of the daughters of Shiloh. . . . And the children of Benjamin did so, and took them wives according to their number of them that danced, whom they caught: and they went and returned into their inheritance, and repaired the cities, and dwelt in them.

Possibly the vine has always been indigenous to Greece. In the forests of Crete wild vines wind among the trees. But legend tells how the vine was brought from the east in early times in the ship of the wine god Dionysus, the mast of which was a vine laden with grapes. In the time of the Homeric heroes, about 1000 BC, wine permeated every part of life all over the Greek world. In the ruins of the Minoan palaces of Knossos in Crete the great stone vats in which the must fermented can still be seen; and on the floor of one of the palaces is the most dramatic wine stain in the world, splashed three and a half thousand years ago, when the Minoan kingdom was destroyed in an unheralded catastrophe, probably a volcanic tidal wave. In the wine cellars of the wise old king Nestor, excavated in 1958, and dating from about 1000 BC, archaeologists found the wine jars ranged in neat rows. The Greeks were very proud of their wine and regarded it as an important aspect of their culture, as is shown in the story of Odysseus and the Cyclops Polyphemus. When Odysseus and his companions found themselves trapped in the cave of the gruesome giant the hero was fortunate enough to have with him a goatskin of dark red wine, a present from a priest of Apollo who had kept it, without his wife's knowledge, in a corner of his cellar. Odysseus offered Polyphemus some of this wine to make him drunk so that the travellers could make good their escape. The Cyclops was enraptured by this excellent Greek wine: '. . . the grain-giving land of the Cyclops also yields them wine of strength, and it is Zeus' rain that waters it for them; but this comes from where ambrosia and nectar flow in abundance.'

Greeks always mixed their wine with a little water in bowls called craters (*krasi*, one of the modern Greek terms for wine, is derived from this word). If contact with the air gave the wine a sharp vinegary taste, honey was added. The cunning inhabitants of Attica devised another method of preserving wine: they sealed the insides of hollowed-out pine trees with a coating of rope fibres steeped in resin. This was certainly ingenious, for resin contains benzoin, a powerful preservative, although the Greeks did not as yet know this. Their light wine kept well, although it tasted strongly of turpentine. They grew so attached to this taste that even today, when the resin is no longer necessary, the light Attic wines are still treated in this way to produce the retsina, famous, if not notorious, with foreign tourists.

Dionysus, the Greek god of wine, was in fact much more than the rollicking flushed-cheeked, nymph-chasing toper that the Renaissance made of him. The Greeks had amazing insight into human psychology and they created two gods for themselves, Apollo and Dionysus, who represented the two poles between which man's life is lived. Apollo was the god of light, the cool, sober intellect, whose principles, inscribed on the temple at Delphi, might be rendered as Know Yourself and Nothing in Excess. But Dionysus was the god of the subconscious, the instinctive, of the impulse and intoxication, and so he became the god of wine. For wine liberates a man from sober reason and intellect and lays bare his innermost self. Or, in the words of the old saying, *in vino veritas* – in wine is truth.

After the Phoenicians the Greeks were the great carriers of the
Mediterranean. They took the famous wines of their islands – those from
Lesbos and Paros were the *grands crus* of that time – to the northern
shores of the Black Sea where the barbarian Scythian kings were glad
enough to set aside their fermented mares' milk for it, and as far as
Spain in the west. They did not need to take wine to Italy for vines
already grew there, as is apparent from an oracle given by a priestess of
Pythian Apollo at Delphi. She urged Greek colonists to beach their boats
'where vine and tree embrace each other in love'. This proved to be the
coast of Italy. Still today in Tuscany and Emilia, vines and trees grow in
this intimate fashion. It was probably the Etruscans, that mysterious
people thought to have come from Asia Minor, who planted the first
vines in Italy. When Romulus and Remus were still drinking the she-wolf's
milk, and the Eternal City had yet to be built on the Seven Hills, the
Etruscans were tending vines on the volcanic hills north of Rome. Wine
entered the gates of Rome at an early date and from the tales of wild
Bacchanalia it is often assumed that the Romans were the grossest of
revellers. There were orgies, of course, and the Romans were coarser
eaters and drinkers than the Greeks ever were; but there were also
Romans who were disgusted by the excesses of the decadent city. Juvenal,
for example, wrote, 'There is no place in my house for these follies. The
clacking of castanets [Spanish dancing girls were very much in the
fashion at that time] and language that is too filthy for whores in stinking
stews is well suited to men who spew wine on floors of Grecian marble.' At
banquets – generally for men – a favourite game was for a diner to drink
as many goblets of wine as there were letters in his mistress's name.
Mistresses with long names must have been much sought after.

When you drink wine in Italy you are drinking history. Virgil, who
had a villa by Lake Garda where he grew lemons, liked to drink the
Valpolicella of that district. When Julius Caesar returned from his
campaigns in Gaul the first thing he wanted after an arduous crossing of
the Alps was a good glass of Barolo from Piedmont. Horace wrote
enthusiastically of the Falerno from the Naples area. Roman snobs,
however, preferred to drink Greek wine, and if this had suffered through
transport by sea, then honey and spices were added, even pepper and salt.
People also attempted to make wine keep better by adding seawater.
Wine was aged by putting amphoras out in the sun, as is still done with
the wines of Frontignan and Banyuls. Wine was often carried in goatskins, a
practice that continues today in places in Greece, and was customary in
sixteenth-century Spain: this is apparent from the story of Don Quixote
who in one incident sets about a row of wineskins in the belief that they are
brigands. Alternatively it could be transported in earthenware amphoras,
tall, narrow jars with handles and a pointed base. In museums you often
see them supported on iron tripods. The pointed bottom, which looks
impractical, had a function: it made the vessels easy to carry on the
shoulder with one finger through a handle, and they could be stacked on

top of each other in ships' holds without much waste of space. The functional virtues of the form are demonstrated by the fact that amphoras are still made on the age-old pattern in Greece, and still used. For storage you simply make a hole in the ground with the point.

When Julius Caesar conquered Gaul, the Romans encountered wooden barrels for the first time, an invention of the Gallic tribes. These Celtic peoples used barrels for beer, for there was no wine yet in western and central Europe, but the Romans soon realized that they were ideal for the transport of wine by ship. The writer Strabo, full of awe, relates: 'Their barrels are bigger than our houses and good pitch helps them caulk these vessels.' A fine relief of a wine ship found at Neumagen and now in the Trier museum shows how barrels of wine were carried down the Moselle sixteen hundred years ago (*see* page 96).

The Greeks introduced the vine into western Europe about 600 BC. The Romans saw to it that it spread further, for the legions had to have wine to sustain their morale, and officials needed it to make life more bearable so far from Rome. Furthermore troops idling on the imperial frontiers had to have something to occupy themselves with (as the emperor Probus said 'I do not feed my soldiers for nothing'), and wine growing was a useful occupation. Thus vineyards were laid out along the furthest frontiers of the Roman empire: in Britain, Champagne, along the Moselle, in Switzerland, along the Danube and by Lake Balaton in Hungary.

But the days of the Roman Empire were numbered: the Huns came riding out of the Asian steppes and all the peoples of Europe, held in an uneasy equilibrium by the Romans, began to move and spill over the frontiers of Imperial Rome. Dark, confused centuries followed when holding on to life and property occupied the whole of people's attention; they had other things than wine to think of. Wine did not, however, vanish completely from men's minds. But it was no longer thought of in the joyous, worldly way of pagan Antiquity, but in terms of the new religion, Christianity, in which this life on earth was no more than transient, a stage on the way to the bliss of the next. Wine acquired a new, profound significance as the blood of Christ. The monasteries that sprang up in France, England, Germany and Switzerland needed wine for the mass and so planting or replanting of vineyards received a great stimulus. In Burgundy the followers of St Bernard built their austere, solid abbeys. They chose where to plant their vines literally by tasting the soil. If it tasted good and pure, they laid out a vineyard. This ancient primitive method can nevertheless hardly be faulted; today the best Burgundies still come from the old monastic vineyards, such as Clos de Vougeot. It was in a French vineyard too that vines are supposed to have been pruned for the first time. According to legend St Martin, bishop of Tours in the fourth century, was riding on his donkey through the vineyards one March morning. So deep in meditation was he that he did not notice that his mount was munching the vine shoots, and great was his dismay when he saw how bare his beast had left them. But in due season it was these denuded vines that had the greatest abundance of grapes and gave the best wine, and since then vines have been pruned each spring.

Orders of nuns, especially in Germany, also occupied themselves with wine growing. In the Rheingau, above Rüdesheim, you can still see the splendid vineyards of the convent where the learned Hildegard of Bingen was abbess in the twelfth century. Hildegard was one of the greatest scholars of her day, with an astounding knowledge of plants and herbs. Not only did she have vineyards laid out, but she brought the Riesling vine to the Rheingau, probably from the Danube valley in Austria – evidence of great perspicacity, for it is in this soil and climate that the Riesling grape produces the finest wines of Germany.

There is no medieval church or cathedral in France without its representations of aspects of wine growing. Everywhere you see vine shoots and leaves, bunches of grapes, grape pickers and wine drinkers on capitals and in stained-glass windows, in the wood carving of choirstalls and the sculptures of façades and porches. These are simple rustic works, often showing a robust, earthy humour – but there are also exalted themes, of Christ as the true vine, and the Passion depicted in terms of grapes that give their blood in the winepress.

Monks, however pious, are only human, and who can blame them for sampling the wines their vineyards brought forth in much larger quantities than were needed for the mass? Certainly not their contemporaries, who may have been a little envious at times, but generally made good-natured fun of the clerical love of wine. There is a student song about Abbot Adam of Angers, of whom it was said that no day went by but that he drank much more than a goodly measure of wine. In Andalusian monasteries the monks slipped frivolous drinking songs in between their chants to enliven the endless offices – in Latin, of course, as this made them less noticeable. One of them has been preserved:

Ave color vini clari, ave sapor sine pari
tua nos inebriari digneris potentia.
Felix venter quem intrabis, felix lingua quem rigabis
felix os quod tu lavabis et beata labia.

(Hail! colour of clear wine, hail peerless taste, you deem us worthy to be made drunk by your power. Happy the belly you enter, happy the tongue you moisten, happy the mouth you lave and blessed the lips.)

The wine that was so enthusiastically drunk in the Middle Ages would not be much appreciated today. It was always drunk young for the bottles and corks necessary for ageing did not exist. It was simply drawn from the barrel until it was empty; this of course brought the wine into contact with the air and often it would have become oxidized and soured. There was good reason for the medieval habit of adding generous quantities of honey and spices, even pepper and salt and seawater. There was another reason for this last ingredient: it gave people such powerful thirsts. Medieval medical science was also much concerned with wine, especially the famed school of Salerno. Until well into the seventeenth century all manner of health rules printed in all kinds of books were attributed to the faculty at Salerno. One example from the Netherlands is dated as late as 1633; it is a verse that appears in a book called *De Borgerlijke Tafel* (The Burgher's Table). It recommends mature, clear wine, to be sipped, not swilled down.

There has always been a great desire for wine in countries where it is too cold to grow the vine – and perhaps for this very reason – and thus wine began to flow in a steady stream from south to north in Europe in the early Middle Ages. At first it was Venetian and Genoese merchant ships that brought Greek and Sicilian wines to the ports of London and Bruges. In the three centuries – from the twelfth to the fifteenth – that Bordeaux and the surrounding country was English, part of the dowry brought by Eleanor of Aquitaine to her marriage to Henry II, the English wine fleet appeared each autumn at Libourne to fetch the claret, the light, red wine of Bordeaux that then made its permanent conquest of English taste. Wine ships, laden with wine from Alsace and the Rhineland, came down the Rhine like the Batavians of old and Dordrecht and Rotterdam became towns of wine merchants. 'Wine thou art green' runs an old Dutch song, and by this was no doubt meant the Riesling from the banks of the Rhine which has a green-gold tint. According to Shakespeare the Duke of Clarence came to a spectacular end in a butt of Malmsey wine, which was a kind of Madeira. Shakespeare himself, and Ben Jonson, probably shared their contemporaries' liking for sherris sack: this was dry sherry, 'sack' being derived from French *sec*. The popularity it acquired in Elizabeth I's time cannot have been diminished by the 3,000 casks that Sir Francis Drake captured on his expedition to Cadiz and bore home in triumph to London.

The taste for particular wines in particular countries sometimes has strange causes. England began to drink port in the early eighteenth century when the country was at war with Louis XIV and imports of French wines ceased. The revocation of the Edict of Nantes by that same monarch, which deprived the Huguenots of their freedom of worship and sent many of them to Holland, was the reason why in the latter country Bergerac and Monbazillac became the favourite wines around 1700. A considerable number of the refugees came from these two places and they maintained their contacts with relations who had stayed behind, most of whom were wine growers. There are still estate owners in Monbazillac whose labels bear the legend *ancien cru hollandais*. Dutch wine merchants set up offices on the Loire, particularly in Anjou. Up to the French Revolution it was Dutchmen who determined the price of Loire wines. And on Sundays cooled Loire wines were drunk in the summer-houses of patrician and merchant dwellings along the Amsterdam canals.

All through these centuries the vines continued to grow and flower in the vineyards of Europe and each autumn new wine was made. In fact there was not much difference between the grape harvests as depicted in that magnificent book of hours, *Les très riches heures du Duc du Berry*, in which we see the pickers at work in the vineyard at the foot of the castle of Saumur, and those of today. Grape picking has always been hard, but jolly work. The gathered grapes are at once a fulfilment and a promise, and the harvest sun is of gold. On 11 November the feast of St Martin was traditionally celebrated with roast goose and the best of the fattened pigs, with fresh nuts and ripe apples, the first cask of new wine was broached and as they drank, the people imbibed warmth, the stored warmth of the summer, and prepared themselves to meet the cold of winter.

The most important period in the history of wine was the seventeenth century. That was when bottles and corks arrived, making it possible for wines of quality to mature to perfection. There were bottles in classical times, and even corks – an amphora from the fifth century BC dug up in Athens was sealed with a cork with a cord through it – but they were not in general use. It is not known who first had the idea of bottling wine, corking it and then leaving it for a period of years. The discovery that wines treated in this way were improved was probably made accidentally. At all events it was from the seventeenth century that people began to experience the wonderful completeness of mature wine, the taste of ancient port, the harmony and balance of venerable Médoc, the golden luxury of an old hock; and, too, the festive bubbling of champagne, for it was cork and bottle that made it possible for the carbon dioxide bubbles produced during fermentation to be retained in the wine. Champagne was yet one more of the gifts of the seventeenth century.

In that century too wineglasses came into general use. The Egyptians had glass but not the technique of glassblowing. This was a Phoenician discovery. The oldest known wineglass dates from the fifth century and was found on the wine island of Samos. It already had the ideal form: a broad bowl, narrowing towards the top, mounted on a foot. Thick glasses of practically the same pattern are still used in small trattorias in working-class districts of Rome. The Romans brought the wineglass to northern Europe; the German rummer, the *Römer*, derives its shape, and probably its name, directly from the wide-bowled Roman wineglass. In the confusion of the migratory period of the fourth and fifth centuries AD such refinements were lost and people drank out of pewter, silver or gold vessels. The Crusaders, however, drank wine from elegant Cypriot and Syrian glasses in Cyprus and the Holy Land, and by this means the wineglass returned to western Europe. But it was still rare and expensive, remaining so when in about 1500 Venice began to give the world its delicate, light-catching wares. It was not until the seventeenth century that increased production of blown glass made the wineglass a household article, albeit still one in the luxury class. To this period belong the beautiful green rummers decorated with vine tendrils, flowers and butterflies and inscribed with suitable devices (*A demain les affaires* is an

Cellarmaster measuring the sugar content of must

example) by daughters of Amsterdam merchants such as Anna Roemer Visser and Maria Tesselschade.

In the seventeenth century the vine conquered the newly discovered world below the equator and across the Atlantic. Jan van Riebeeck welcomed French Huguenots to Cape Colony to found and tend vineyards; Spanish monks planted vineyards in South America and California.

If the seventeenth century was a glorious one for wine, the nineteenth was tragic. It was then that the small, beetle-like phylloxera appeared, a parasite that lives in the roots of the vine and has acquired the evil sobriquet of *vastatrix*, the destroyer. It arrived in Europe in 1863, probably in an American seaman's kit. In 1869 it appeared in Bordeaux, in 1870 it was reported in Portugal, in 1892 in Champagne and in 1904 in Jerez. Slowly but inexorably the vineyards died across Europe as far as modern Yugoslavia. No remedy was found until someone had the idea of grafting European quality vines onto the roots of wild American stock, which was immune to the phylloxera. This proved to be where salvation lay and the practice was adopted in nearly all European vineyards. There were just a few exceptions – here and there in Hungary, on the Moselle and in the Palatinate (Rheinpfalz), and even a few small vineyards in Bordeaux. For a long time the finest example of a pre-phylloxera vineyard was La Romanée-Conti in Burgundy, but after World War II its vines too were grafted onto American stock.

35

Modern methods of cultivation in a vineyard

Today tastes in wine have developed and become more sophisticated, but in a world growing ever more hectic and superficial with less and less time and patience to spare. Large machines, on wheels high enough to enable them to straddle the rows of vines, now work the vineyards. If hailstorms threaten rockets can be fired into the clouds to change the hail into rain. In wineries rattling *égrappeurs* strip the grapes from their stalks and horizontal winepresses rotate. In the cellars of the big cooperatives young wine ferments in enormous tanks of 14,000 litres capacity or even more. In laboratories oenologists bend over test tubes of wine and must to fathom the last secrets of fermentation, or to find cures for wine diseases and to improve quality.

It is the simple wines in particular that have benefited from these innovations. The great wines are mostly still made by the traditional craft methods: although today many châteaux of repute have cellarmasters with academic qualifications in oenology; and even with good wines the skins are now left for a shorter period to ferment with the must, to make the wine lighter and ready for drinking sooner. A Burgundy of today tastes quite different from a pre-war one. The heavy old Burgundies that our grandfathers waxed lyrical over exist no more. We no longer have the patience to leave wines to mature over a long period; we want to drink our wine as soon as possible. In addition there are now many more people who can afford wine and who want to drink it. But new vineyards cannot be started just anywhere, for soil and climate are not everywhere suitable. The great wines therefore are becoming steadily more expensive, as always happens when demand increases but supply perforce remains limited. However, thanks to scientific and technological advance all manner of small, simple wines that formerly attracted little attention and were not highly appreciated outside their home districts have been so improved that they can absorb some at least of the new demand. Science and technology have put a growing range of well-made, moderately priced, agreeable wines of a decent average quality, with the light, not-too-serious character we appreciate today, within reach of more people than ever before. Romantic souls no doubt feel some nostalgia for the old dark cellars where the grapes were trodden by foot, for the days when cellarmasters put their ears to casks to listen to the progress of fermentation or considered the state of the moon to see if it was time to bottle the wine. Happily this romantic aura has not entirely departed.

However, if we are honest, there is reason to rejoice at the increased scope that maker and buyer now have. For wine is wine and remains a true companion, however times may change. And every honest wine is a joy for the heart and a solace for the spirit.

The drinking of wine

Some time ago a magnum of Château Mouton-Rothschild 1928 was
auctioned in London for several thousand pounds. The bottle went
to the United States and the new owner told the journalists who hastened
to interview him that he did not yet know what he was going to do with it.
Probably this venerable magnum of one of the world's best wines from
one of the century's best vintages has ended up in a place of honour in a
curio cabinet and no one will ever drink it. This is a tragedy, for the wine
has missed its destiny. There is only one way in which wine can fulfil its
purpose, and that is for it to be drunk and enjoyed by someone. Therefore
everything that is ever spoken or written about wine boils down to one
question: how does a particular wine measure up to its task of affording a
few hours' delight? As all happiness in life consists of some form of
exchange, we must also ask ourselves what we can do to give wine its
chance of successfully fulfilling its function. For pleasure, like everything
else, has to be merited. Wine has to be treated with loving care if it is to
present itself at its best; and we have to meet it half way, as it were, and
approach it in a receptive frame of mind, ready to experience and savour
all the properties that make it worth while. This is the secret of intelligent
wine drinking, of prime importance for the great wines, but not without
relevance to the lesser ones. Every wine deserves to be judged on its merits,
every wine should be given a fair chance. This is not affectation, still less
snobbery; it is quite simply part of the art of living, and that implies
enjoying all life's gifts – in the true sense of the word for what they are
worth. And part of that art may lie in not taking life's graver matters more
seriously than they deserve, and in taking less serious matters – such as
wine – with greater seriousness than they sometimes receive.

Wine is part of our culture and has evolved with it, and it follows the
perpetual pendulum swings of style and taste. We drink and appreciate
different wines from our forefathers. In the Middle Ages people drank
whatever wine happened to be to hand. They did not bother very much
about what wine they served with salmon or game or roasted ox. It might
be hot wine with honey and spices. Nevertheless we should not dismiss
this as a barbarous period. Erasmus, for example, devoted a book to

38

education, *De civilitate morum puerilium*, and in it he wrote that the lips should be wiped with a napkin before drinking and that one should drink delicately, not 'slurping with a noise like a horse'. Seventeenth-century books of etiquette laid down rules for behaviour at table and for drinking wine. *De Borgerlijke Tafel* of 1633, referred to above, exhorted its readers to drink in a seemly fashion, and never when their mouths were full.

There is little trace, however, of any appreciation of wine in the proper sense in that age, although it should be pointed out that certain combinations of food and wine were being observed: it was in the seventeenth century that, for example, Chablis came to be associated with oysters.

It was not until about 1800 that the rules of wine drinking as we accept them today began to take form. The French writer and connoisseur Grimod de la Reynière was one of the first men to serve wines in a planned sequence and to give thought to their combination with particular dishes. His arch-enemy, the diplomatist Talleyrand, of whom it was said that he liked light women and heavy wines, was the man who laid down what has since become the classic rule for tasting wine. He said that the glass should first be held up to the light, to enjoy the shining, scintillating colour and deep glow. Then the wine should be swirled gently round the glass so that it yields its deepest fragrance, and this is evaluated and savoured with the nostrils held over the rim of the glass. After this the glass should be put down so that the wine can be discussed. And when all its beauties and promise have been picked out and talked over comes the moment to taste it, letting it pass from left to right and from front to back in the mouth.

In the course of the nineteenth century the rules for pairing wines with particular dishes were established: white wine with fish and hors d'oeuvres, red wine with meat, sweet wine with sweet desserts. But just as traditional folk music is not bound by the rules of classical music, so in countries where wine is produced and people daily drink their own simple local product, no one troubles himself too much with the orthodox rules. In the Balkans people drink white wine in the summer and red in the winter, regardless of the food that is being served; on the coasts of Spain they drink their local red wine with fish, crustaceans and shellfish; and in parts of central Europe where only white wine is made, this is drunk with wild boar if needs be.

People in wine-importing countries have so wide a choice that they can select the perfect wine for a particular moment, a particular dish and a particular mood and atmosphere. And that is no small privilege.

Buying wine

There are many ways of tackling the buying of wine. You could, like prosperous citizens of old, invite your wine merchant to call once or twice a year and walk him round the racks in your cellar, noting where replenishment is required and then, over port and cigars, discuss vintages and make up the order, of so much Château this, so much Château that. Or you can, on arriving home to the smell of chicken roasting in the kitchen, rush out and buy a bottle of table wine. Between these two extremes, of which the first belongs to a different world from ours, and the second is a shade too casual, there are many possible courses. Laying in your own stock of wine, however modest, is a source of much pleasure. Few people today when flats and houses are usually small can possess a wine cellar of their own, but it may be possible to find a corner somewhere for four or even six dozen bottles. Of course there is little point in using up precious storage space for run-of-the-mill table wines. These can be bought for immediate consumption as required. But buying young wines of good quality that are going to be worth the trouble and effort of ageing them to perfection in your own 'cellar' is a wonderfully rewarding hobby. There is a lot of satisfaction to be had in the knowledge that there in the cool darkness are a number of bottles improving with age against the time when they will afford an evening of informed pleasure.

Most wine merchants give ample information about the character and potential of the wines on their lists so that the customer can have some idea in advance whether wines he has not tried before are likely to suit his style and taste. When buying wines for your own stock in this way there is no skill or virtue in simply laying in the expensive kinds, even supposing you have the money to do so; although you are of course absolutely safe with classified *crus* from the Médoc or St-Emilion or famous Burgundies. The real pleasure comes from making discoveries among the middle-priced wines. All you need is a willingness to venture. It is also a good idea to include in your stock wines such as Beaujolais, rosés, simple German kinds, and of course sherry and port, which always come in useful for enlivening those evenings when friends have to be entertained at short notice. Wines of so-called lesser vintages can often be just as agreeable in their way as those of the great years. And it is among

Parisian wine shop

unfamiliar wines, not burdened with great reputations to live up to, that the most surprising discoveries can be made. You need to have a modicum of intuition, a little experience of, and feeling for, wine, and in addition you have to be able to read and interpret wine labels.

All that can be discerned from the outside of a bottle of wine is the colour of its contents, red, white or rosé; the rest at this stage is an enigma. For this reason bottles are provided with labels to describe, or at least to state their contents. Now it would of course be possible to design labels purely on the decorative principle and to apply them at random. This would be fraudulent and a breach of the laws governing such matters in most countries. In fact this sort of thing goes on much less than suspicious wine drinkers might sometimes suppose. Wine-producing countries protec their wine and therefore, by extension, the customer. The latter's task is to learn to deduce from the label how far this protection extends and what he may expect from the wine. It is fortunately quite easy to learn to interpret wine labels.

Let us begin with French wines. If the label confines itself to announcin a pretty name, perhaps preceded by 'château' and ornamented by an accompanying view, or the words *grand vin* are printed but no indication of native commune or district, or perhaps at most the name of a wine merchant in a particular wine region, then all the label quarantees is that you are buying wine, made from grapes, with an alcoholic strength of at least 9 per cent. 'French' wines of such anonymity do not necessarily even come from France. They need not be bad; they are just very simple wines of which not too much should be expected.

Matters are improved if the region of origin is named on the label (Côtes de Provence for instance) with in addition the letters VDQS, which stand for *vin délimité de qualité supérieure*. This guarantees that the wir comes from the region named and fulfils certain requirements with regard to type of grape, vinification and so on. There are about sixty VDQS wines in France, of which many – those of Lorraine for example – are seldom encountered outside the country. The VDQS grading is taken very seriously in France.

The most familiar French designation of quality is the *appellation contrôllée* (AC). It is often forgotten that each AC stands by itself and that the French wine laws may impose higher standards of quality on one AC than another. Generally speaking, however, the smaller the area covered by a given AC, the higher the standards the wine must satisfy. Thus in Bordeaux the 'AC Bordeaux' designates the cheapest of its wines; above this comes the AC of the region (such as Médoc, Sauternes); and above that the AC of the commune (Margaux, St-Estèphe, Moulis and so on).

If in addition to the AC of a commune the label carries the name of the vineyard or château with the owner's name, then you are sure of a wine of very good quality and you can also be absolutely sure of its

Three types of German wine label:
Qualitätswein
Deutscher Tafelwein (German table wine)
Qualitätswein mit Prädikat (superior wine with specification of quality)

precise origin. If the words *mise du château* or *mis en bouteilles au château* appear on the label this means that the wine was bottled in its native cellar. This is a good guarantee of reliability, but it does not necessarily mean that the contents are any better than the same wine bottled in the importing country. However, there is an increasing tendency in France for wine to be exported in the bottle, including wines that do not come from a château, so as to offer a maximum guarantee as far as origin is concerned. In this case the label, or the cork, bears the legend *mis en bouteilles dans la région de production*.

Any wine of any consequence should also carry the year of its vintage.

In recent years more and more labels have been appearing which indicate the place of origin of the wine, usually naming the district and sometimes the commune, and also give the brand name of a wine firm, but do not state a vintage. Wines labelled in this way generally consist of a blend of wine of various years and a number of vineyards within an AC area. Quite often too these are wines that could normally claim a higher appellation but because of particular circumstances, such as a bad year, they have been declassified. Such wines are mostly of a reasonable, average quality. So for a moderate price you get a decent wine with the brand name as a guarantee. The name of the firm that markets these wines is important: well-known houses have a reputation to lose and they are therefore careful to see that their stock in trade comes up to a good standard.

There is usually quite a lot to read on German wine labels, even when the wine is a modest one. The cheapest of all generally carry only a rather romantic name, with perhaps the name of a *Grosskellerei*. These vague intimations tell the buyer nothing, not even the origin of the wines labelled in this manner. They are nearly always lowly white wines, often from one of the Balkan countries. If a German wine is of any importance at all the label carries the name of the commune (in most cases with an -er added to make the place name into an adjective), followed by the *Lage* (the site or vineyard), as for example Bernkasteler Doktor, Rüdesheimer Rosengarten. Great confusion has arisen in the naming of German wines, however, because it has become customary for a variety of wines from a particular commune to bear the name of its most famous site. The result is that a description such as Niersteiner Domthal or Zeller Schwarze Katz no longer means what it seems to say. (Liebfraumilch too: it is said originally to have come from a vineyard belonging to a church at Worms, the Liebfrauenkirche, but it is now merely a generic term for a type of wine.) Such names are just a general indication of wine from a certain district, but of rather moderate quality. To introduce some order into the chaos occasioned by this practice Germany has brought in a new system, in force since the 1971 grape harvest (*see* page 158).

Since late 1971 all German wine labels have carried official designations of quality: *Deutscher Tafelwein* or *Tischwein* (German table wine), for example, with the addition only of the district of origin for the lowest grade; *Qualitätswein* with the name of the commune, site and variety of grape for wines of medium quality; and *Qualitätswein mit Prädikat*, followed by name of commune, site and type of grape for the very good wines. These classifications guarantee a specific standard of quality; the wine in the bottle has passed an inspection before they are given. This is different in principle from the position in France, where a wine receives its *appelatio contrôllée* if it fulfils the appropriate requirements laid down for the particular AC area, with regard to grape variety, vinification, alcoholic strength and so on; in other words it conforms to a local, not a national standard. German labels often carry an indication of the ripeness of the grapes when they were picked, for example *Spätlese* (late-gathered bunches); *Auslese* (selected fully ripe bunches); *Beerenauslese* (selected fully ripe grapes); and *Trockenbeerenauslese* (selected shrivelled grapes). The description *naturrein* (natural, pure), which means that no sugar has been added to the wine, will in future be omitted: all *Qualitätsweine mit Prädikat* are *naturrein*. The EEC has been working for some years to order the wine market in such a way that all member countries will be obliged to respect each other's wine laws and regulations.

As far as wine from countries other than France and Germany is concerned it is always wise to look for labels that give the greatest possible amount of information. Generally speaking the less information a label gives the less guarantee it is likely to offer of its contents. It is always a good idea to buy wine that frankly states the details of its origin, however modest and unglamorous.

STORAGE

Bottles of wine should always be stored lying down, so that the cork remains moist: this ensures that the bottle is effectively sealed. Wine has to be in contact with the air if it is to age, but the porosity of the cork is sufficient for this purpose. If the wine gets too much air it will oxidize and spoil. This is easily detected: the wine takes on a brownish tinge. The ideal place for storing wine is of course a cellar where it is dark and still (preferably not near to a busy road) and where the temperature does not fall below 8°C in the winter, nor rise above 16°C in the summer. An ideal temperature would be one that remains between 10 and 12°C throughout the year. If the cellar is too warm the wine matures too quickly; if it is too cold the wine makes no headway at all. If you have an old-fashioned cellar and can set a part of it aside for the purpose, the best plan is to run up some wooden racks for the bottles, with upright partitions if necessary to stop the bottles from rolling about.

There are also good, easily installed metal racks made. They are widely used in the wine trade. The bottles are laid label uppermost and the bottom to the outside so that the labels can be read. If you have a large stock you can write names and vintages on cards hung on the racks.

If you do not possess a cellar you will have to improvise. There is usually some corner of wasted space in a house – although it should be

44

remembered that central heating may make the temperature too high for keeping wine for very long. No real disasters are likely to occur in six months, but if you want to store wines over a period of years the temperature must not be too high, or white wines will certainly suffer.

For small improvised wine corners – in a cupboard or on a landing – you can buy handy metal racks for a dozen or two dozen bottles in the shops. Larger sizes are available, but these unfortunately are not very stable and the wine will be subject to too much harmful vibration, especially if the racks stand near a much-used passage or stairs.

You can also install a small, decorative wooden rack in your living room for keeping a few bottles of red wine at room temperature ready to serve.

TASTING

The worst thing we can do to wine is to drink it unheedingly. In doing so we are not only being unfair to the wine, but also to ourselves, for we are missing one of the most refined, subtle and intelligent pleasures that life has to offer. Wine is not so much for drinking in the mundane sense as for tasting and enjoying (although exception should be made here for all those pleasant, unpretentious little wines that are indeed drunk to assuage thirst, in large draughts and without further thought). And the more consciously you drink wine the greater the pleasure. There is no great magical secret involved in becoming knowledgeable about wine, no special native talent is required. Knowledge of wine is something you acquire, pleasurably, with each glass that you drink with awareness, receptive to everything the wine has to offer. One thing that must be put aside is that inhibiting fear of becoming or appearing affected or snobbish. There can be no snobbery in savouring such an enchanting gift of nature combined with the experience and skill of men. Judgment and enjoyment of wine still depend on the three stages Talleyrand prescribed for his guests before they drank his undoubtedly excellent wines; the three stages that were summed up in Hungarian wine cellars by the letters COS: *color, odor, sapor* (taste), the Latin words used for the sake of foreign buyers who spoke no Hungarian.

Anyone who is at all serious about the task of drinking and appreciating wine starts by holding it up against the light, for preference the soft, living light of a candleflame (never ever attempt to judge wine in a room lit by fluorescent lamps for these make the best wine look like a nasty syrup). In suitable light the wine appears alive and glowing, and the beholder can take pleasure in its fire, its depth and splendour of colour. It goes without saying that the wine must be clear. Cloudy wine is undrinkable. Apart from the aesthetic pleasure that is derived from the appearance of clear wine, colour also reveals much of its quality. There are white wines – examples are Chablis, Pouilly-Fuissé, German Rieslings and Alsatian wines – that have a greenish tint in their gold, and this is indicative of their high quality. Sweet white wines, such as Sauternes, Tokays, and *Trockenbeerenauslesen* from the Rhine districts, have a deep amber glow; wines of the Loire like Sancerre and Pouilly-Fumé have a warm, sunny quality to their golden colour. Moselle wines shine like a fresh March sun and a good white Graves has a hint of topaz. Beware of white wines with a brownish tinge: they are either too old or have been carelessly kept; at all events their day is past.

The nuances of colour in red wine are endless: from the bright clear red of a fruity young Beaujolais to the deep, secretive amethyst glow of a mature Hermitage; from the dark smouldering red of a St-Emilion to the splendid ruby scintillation of a Médoc. Very young red wines still have the pinkish hue of the newly pressed must. They are too young to be really good and need to mature for several years more. A Beaujolais with a tinge of pink has a good dash of something of different provenance in the bottle. As the years advance a red wine loses its purplish glow and its red deepens. This means that the wine is mature and has acquired character. It takes longer for this depth of colour to be achieved in wine from a great year than in those of lesser years; but the better the vintage the deeper and more luxurious the colour, the more it seems to sparkle and gleam. This rich, vital colour indicates a wine at the height of its development. As the wine grows older there appears in the strong red colour, almost imperceptibly at first, a golden tinge, noticeable when you look into the surface of the wine. The wine at this stage may still be excellent, mild in taste and with an infinitely subtle bouquet, in which new nuances are constantly discovered. If the wine becomes older still then slowly but

46

surely it begins to lose strength, that touch of gold turns to brown and if you look into the surface of the wine you detect a pale, anaemic border around the inside of the glass. The wine becomes thin, but remarkably enough it often retains its aroma. It has become as it were spiritualized and will shortly die and turn watery. Exactly when this will happen cannot be forecast. It cannot be said with certainty of any wine how old it can or should become. The author has drunk Beaujolais – said not to have a long life – more than ten years old, and it was excellent. As a general rule it can be said that clarets, especially Médocs of good provenance and vintage, can reach a quarter century and more. Red Burgundies usually do not manage this; about fifteen years would be the maximum for many of them. White wines, with a few exceptions such as Sauternes, hocks and Tokays, do not age. They are best drunk young, although an old white Burgundy can be something rather special. Fortified wines such as port, sherry and Madeira, can easily reach a century, the good ones at least.

After the colour there is the aroma of wine to be savoured. The glass should be gently rotated so that the wine swirls around it and releases its fragrance, its nose as the expert calls it. The nose of a wine can be the subject of endless discussion, so interesting is it, so much pleasure does it afford. The light but penetrating scent of flowers of a Riesling wine. The woodland scents of rich red wines of the Côte de Nuits in which you can sometimes detect a hint of blackberries or bilberries, or the famed wood violet perfume of the wines of Musigny. The fruity scent of a good Beaujolais suggesting raspberries, or apples or strawberries. The raspberry aroma of red wines from Bourgueil and the pronounced spiciness of Côtes du Rhône; the smell of almonds in a Meursault; the faint hint of salt sea air in a Muscadet. The camomile fragrance of a Manzanilla sherry and the luxuriousness of an old port. The aristocratic perfume of champagne and the infinitely complicated and distinguished nose of a fine Médoc. Savouring the fragrances of a glass of wine is a subtle and refined pleasure: how often do we really use our sense of smell?

Then after we have lingered over colour and scent we take the first draught – truly a draught, not a diffident sip – which can be rolled round the mouth, from front to back and from side to side, over and under the tongue. This is the aspect that is so vital a part of the true appreciation of wine. Wine can be dry or sweet, filling the mouth with richness. It can be gentle and modest, it can taste proud and aristocratic, or hot and full of temperament. There is wine like liquid fire, or wine that is benignly cool and fresh. Then after the wine is swallowed there comes the aftertaste. It may be light and delicate; it may go on to reveal seven more aftertastes. No one should be afraid to search for words to describe the tastes of wine; they can be found, for wine makes a poet of the most matter-of-fact of souls. When we have learned to recognize wines, it is all rather like meeting old friends. We prove again how different the robustness of a St-Emilion is from the robustness of a Côtes du Rhône; the elegance of a Médoc from the elegance of a Beaune.

Wine and gastronomy

The correct combination of wine and food is often regarded as a difficult and complicated matter, full of traps and pitfalls, and gaffes for the making. For this reason people sometimes resort to rosés on the grounds that these at least 'go with anything'. This is a great pity, for although a rosé may be generally and inoffensively suitable, the combination is usually far from interesting. If wine and food are well matched they flatter each other: the food tastes better and more satisfying and complete, and unsuspected qualities are revealed in the wine. If you are serving a dish with a rich sauce, or one consisting of roast meat, or delicate fish, then it is a downright sin in these circumstances to fall back on anything as all-purpose as a rosé. (An exception can be made here for a rosé like a Tavel, which tastes splendid with any dish to which garlic has been liberally added.) For the successful matching of wine and food, all that is needed is understanding and taste, and of course the measure of imagination necessary to tell in advance the effect of certain combinations.

If more than one wine is to be served in the course of a meal or an evening's entertaining then it is only logical to begin with the lightest, the youngest, and then to work towards a climax. We start a meal with soup or hors d'oeuvres and progress towards the main dish, and the wine should proceed parallel with this sequence. Modern ideas on this subject are different from those of people in Biblical times, as the story of the wedding feast at Cana shows. When Christ turned the water into wine which proved to be better than what had previously been offered, surprise was expressed that the bridegroom had served the lesser wine first – the normal course of events for us.

That red wine is not drunk with fish is perfectly understandable: the tannin it contains clashes with fish – except, that is, when the fish has been cooked in red wine. In France they do this with sole in Burgundy, with lampreys in St-Emilion, and eels are cooked in this way along the Loire. Today we no longer serve a heavy, sweet wine such as Sauternes with fish, as was customary fifty years ago. Our style of life is quicker-paced than that of our forebears, we eat less heavily and our taste is less for luxurious wines than for the light, young ones. But just for this reason it is a good idea sometimes to try a Sauternes or a *Spätlese* from the Rhine

Goat's milk cheeses with white wine

with the richer kind of fish dish such as sole à la meunière or turbot in cloudy Hollandaise sauce.

No one should be timid when it comes to choosing wine. Red wine certainly goes with good red meat or game, but in Alsace and along the Rhine, where they have excellent game but hardly any local red wine, they drink a full-bodied white, Tokay d'Alsace for instance, or a wine from the Palatinate. If the game has been marinaded in white wine this can make an interesting combination.

Above all it should not be thought that wine can only be drunk with festive meals, or that it must always be expensive. An ordinary roast chicken on Sunday will be all the better for a glass of wine – a Spanish

49

Rioja, a Beaujolais or one of those pleasant, spicy wines from Corbières. And a glass of wine tastes better than might be imagined with the homeliest of casseroles. The city of Bremen gives a banquet every year for the ships' captains and owners who bring wealth to this north German port. The menu for this festive occasion is cabbage and sausage and bacon, and with it they drink a decent Rhine wine. Once in a while try a modest white wine with sauerkraut or mussels; or an ordinary red with goulash or cold meats. A fresh, slightly tart Moselle is also good with cooked meats, and a cooled rosé goes well with curries. Good plain farmhouse cooking requires sturdy, no-nonsense wines, preferably with *terroir*, a suggestion of earthiness.

Never drink a subtly fragrant wine with a strongly spiced dish because it would be totally overwhelmed. Similarly a wine with a delicate bouquet does not marry with strongly smelling cheeses; a young fruity wine is needed here. Mild, creamy cheeses go best with high-class mature wines. It is always a good plan to combine dishes and wines from the same region. Dishes with a markedly Mediterranean flavour, with a lot of garlic, tomatoes and herbs, demand one of the hot-blooded wines of Spain or the south of France. An Alsatian or German wine goes with sauerkraut. Wines from the great rivers, such as the Loire and the Rhine, balance river fish such as salmon, eel or, for those who like it, pike. Red or white Bordeaux taste excellent with pâté, a dish that came originally from southwest France.

Whatever your approach to the question, whatever combinations you favour, wine will always add a festive note even to the homeliest and simplest meal. An evening with friends in your home takes on an extra dimension, added conviviality if you serve them wine. In combining food and wine you can start with a dish and then choose a suitable wine to accompany it. But it can be much more exciting to start with the wine, as long as you are not afraid to experiment. Who would imagine, for example, that a bone-dry Muscat d'Alsace would taste so splendid with pâté, or a dry Madeira? Or that fresh new season's herring and a light, dry sherry would make such a good pair? Or white Bordeaux and a sweetish Emmenthal or Gruyère? Or a fresh white cheese like a Gervais and a rosé, or some types of Dutch cheese with a Moselle?

Always be careful to let your wine be at its best: the white cool but not ice-cold; the red brought slowly to room temperature (at least a day in a warm room), and remember too that all wines, even the humblest, are better for being served in a large glass half filled. How otherwise can it be swirled around in the glass so that it releases its fragrances?

More guidance on matching wines with food will be found on page 158.

Wine regions of the world

On the following pages are descriptions of wines and wine regions, together with maps of those regions. Maps are an important aid when it comes to wine: from them you can see how particular districts and vineyards are situated with regard to the sun, to rivers, hillsides and lakes. Situation is of the greatest importance for the character and quality of the wine. The maps also show where the great wine centres lie and too all the wine villages with their world-famous names. The wine lover pays careful attention to maps for they can tell him so much about wine.

Anyone likely to pass near one of these wine regions in the course of a journey can use these maps to plan a visit. Drive to the wine region, but once you are there leave your car somewhere. You should walk through vineyards, feeling beneath your feet the ground in which the vines put down their roots, touching the tender leaves or, when the grapes are ripe on the vines, picking and sampling a bunch. You should 'read' the following maps as if you were walking through the vineyards and hearing the leaves rustle in the wind.

30°

30°

50°

As can be seen from this map, the wine-growing areas of the world lie mainly between latitudes 30° and 50°

WORLD WINE PRODUCTION IN HECTOLITRES, 197

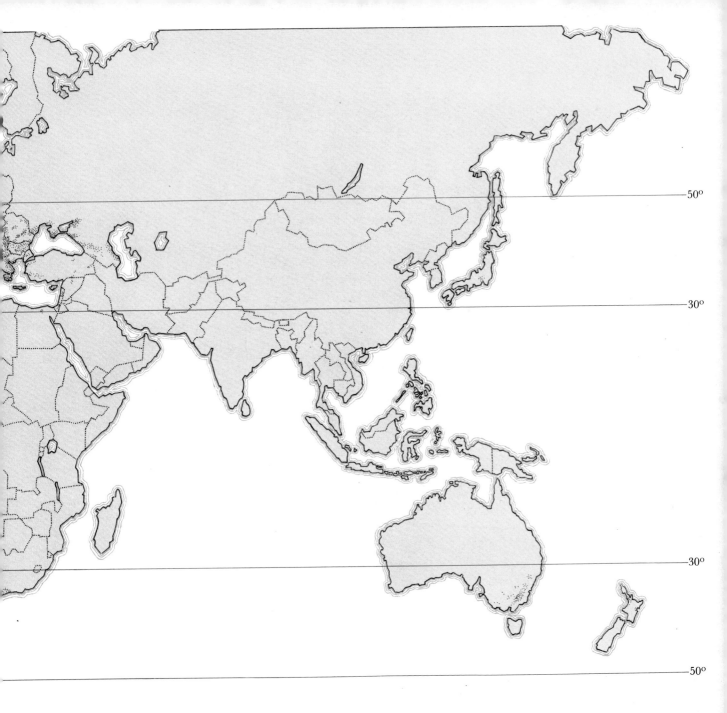

Algeria	8,000,000 hl	Chile	4,000,000 hl	Italy	63,700,000 hl	South Africa	5,800,000 hl
Argentina	23,000,000 hl	Cyprus	1,200,000 hl	Lebanon	45,000 hl	Spain	41,000,000 hl
Australia	2,500,000 hl	France	61,000,000 hl	Luxembourg	100,000 hl	Switzerland	880,000 hl
Austria	1,800,000 hl	Germany	6,000,000 hl	Morocco	1,100,000 hl	Tunisia	1,000,000 hl
Belgium	10,000 hl	Greece	5,000,000 hl	Netherlands	10,000 hl	United States	14,000,000 hl
Brazil	2,000,000 hl	Hungary	4,400,000 hl	Portugal	9,000,000 hl	USSR	29,000,000 hl
Bulgaria	4,300,000 hl	Israel	400,000 hl	Rumania	7,700,000 hl	Yugoslavia	4,200,000 hl

53

France

Of the eighty-nine French *départements* there are only seven where no vines grow: in the extreme north and along the damp, chilly Channel coast. They are present everywhere else. In winter they gleam black and wet, pruned back to their gnarled stems, standing in sodden clay or among the stones and gravel. In the spring the buds swell and with the first warm April days each bud reveals a small, downy light-green shoot that grows into tender leaves in the caressing spring sunshine, so that it looks as if the gnarled and knotted old vines have been hung with a veil of green gauze. In June come the fragrant green-yellow flowers which soon turn into hard, green incipient fruit. In the warm days of August the bunches of grapes form which by the end of September hang heavy and sweet among the leaves ready for the pickers. And when in mid-October the young wine is fermenting in the cellars the vineleaves begin to turn to gold, vermilion, bronze and deep purple – the colours of wine – and then it is as if the vineyards had been swathed in brocade. When November and its mists arrives the vines stand dark and gnarled and shiny again, waiting for the spring.

France is a land of wine, from cool Champagne to the hot Midi, from convivial Alsace to reserved Bordeaux, from Burgundy to the Pyrenees, from the banks of the Loire to those of the Rhône. Everywhere wine, from the costly, aristocratic Bordeaux to the humble Provençal, from the dry, light Muscadet to the heavy golden Sauternes, from the rich, luxurious Burgundies to the more astringent Alsatians, from festive, sparkling champagne to dark Rhône wines, from jovial Beaujolais to reserved Médoc.

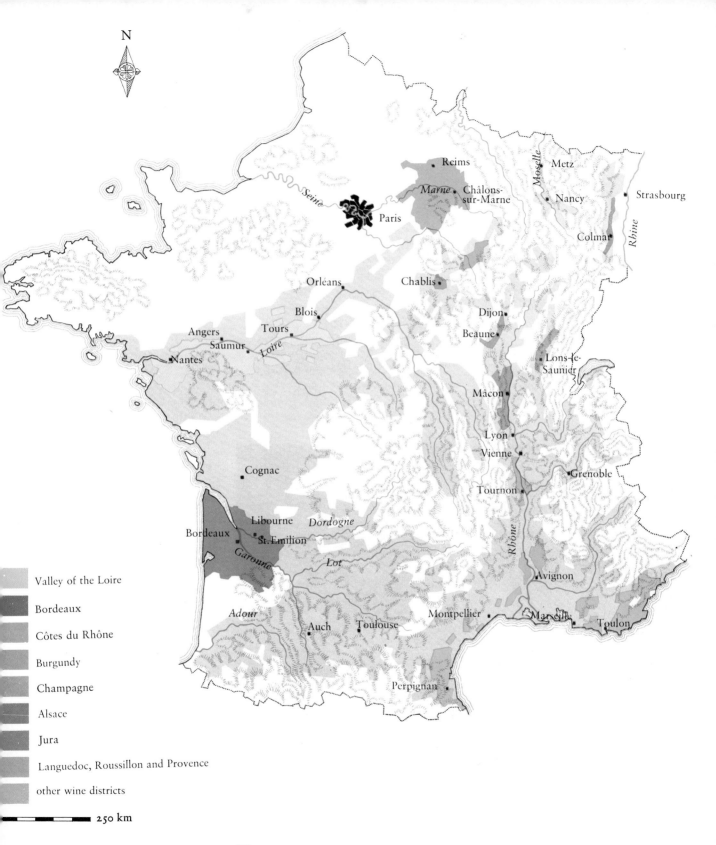

N

Valley of the Loire

Bordeaux

Côtes du Rhône

Burgundy

Champagne

Alsace

Jura

Languedoc, Roussillon and Provence

other wine districts

250 km

Reims

Marne

Châlons-
sur-Marne

Moselle

Metz

Nancy

Strasbourg

Colmar

Rhine

Paris

Seine

Orléans

Chablis

Dijon

Beaune

Lons-le-
Saunier

Blois

Tours

Angers

Saumur

Loire

Nantes

Mâcon

Lyon

Vienne

Grenoble

Cognac

Tournon

Libourne

Dordogne

Bordeaux

St. Emilion

Garonne

Lot

Rhône

Avignon

Adour

Auch

Toulouse

Montpellier

Marseille

Toulon

Perpignan

Bordeaux

The wine districts of Bordeaux, the *régions* as the French term them, radiate out from the old port like the petals of a flower. Clockwise from northeast to northwest they are Côte de Blaye, Côte de Bourg, Fronsac, Pomerol, St-Emilion, Côtes de Bordeaux, Entre-deux-Mers, Sauternes, Graves and Médoc. All the wines from these districts are Bordeaux, but each district has given a unique character to its wine. This character is closely bound up with the composition of the soil, the amount of humidity, situation with regard to the sun, the type of grape that does best in the particular soil conditions, and with old traditions of winemaking. No wineland of France offers such a great diversity as Bordeaux, from the very humble to the highest-ranking aristocrats of wine, from deep, glowing red to straw yellow, from the driest of dry to honey sweet, from the robustly masculine to the gracefully feminine, everything a winelover might dream of. Ordinary Bordeaux wines are entitled only to the appellation 'Bordeaux', sometimes followed by 'Supérieur' if they come above a certain alcoholic strength. The next category is identified by one of the districts listed above, and the best Bordeaux is labelled with the commune of origin. Bordeaux wines traditionally carry the name of a château. The name of a château on a label does not mean much in itself. Only the appellation is of real significance since every owner of vineyards and a *chai* can call his villa or estate a château. There are about 10,000 châteaux in the districts around Bordeaux. A number of these, not more than about two hundred, produce wine of a quality that has brought them fame, sometimes a world reputation, and in such cases the château name obviously means a great deal. A wine that bears a famous name is a matter of pride and honour to the owner. He guarantees the wine with his name and imposes on himself even higher standards than are officially required. To preserve their reputations many of these famous châteaux market wines pseudonymously or under a brand name if they are of a not too successful vintage, or if they have been made from young vines.

'Knights' of Sauternes

Grapes arriving at a chai

In 1855 an official classification was drawn up for the best Médoc wines. Sixty Médocs and one red Graves which closely approached the Médocs in character were divided into a system ranging through five grades of *crus* or growths. This classification does not, as is often thought, depend on one particular test of quality but was originally worked out on the basis of the aggregate of the prices these top wines had fetched in the previous years. In broad outline the system remains a just one today, although there are several châteaux that, because of improvement in quality, perhaps should now be entitled to a higher classification and others that no longer merit their original grading. The *premiers crus* come at the top of this hierarchically arranged classification and represent the highest degree of excellence attainable in French wines (*see* table, page 155).

Immediately after them come a number of *crus bourgeois*, the solid burghers of Bordeaux; these are very good wines, some of which should, in the judgment of many people, be placed in the higher category.

The wines of Sauternes are also officially classified: one *grand premier cru* (Château d'Yquem) and a number of first and second *crus*; and Graves, St-Emilion and Pomerol all have a number of wines entitled to the classification *grand cru*.

Unfortunately these two upper classes among French wines are unavoidably expensive. The vineyards where the great wines are grown cannot be extended: the quality and character of the wines is the product of their particular plot of ground, its position, and soil composition; and also these wines are still made by the traditional craftsman's methods. Fortunately these top classes are followed by many well-made, honest and often really fine wines that are sold at reasonable prices.

Every winelover can find in the *chais*, the wineries-cum-cellars of Bordeaux, a wine that exactly suits him. Bordeaux wines are therefore excellent for matching with food. There is no conceivable dish for which a Bordeaux could not be found elegantly to accompany it. They are splendid wines for drinking, not at noisy parties, but quietly of an evening with a few good friends, sampling them with cheese, nuts, and perhaps some pâté. Bordeaux wines, whether expensive or moderately priced, can never be dull. It is worth remembering too that claret is the most healthful of wines; that it keeps people young is shown by the many golden weddings celebrated in this much-blessed part of France.

Bordeaux : West

MÉDOC

North of Bordeaux along the broad Gironde lies the narrow strip called the Médoc. It is flat country with here and there a hill, some sparse conifer woods, with sands and gravels in which glittering quartz is sometimes found, on a subsoil of clay. It is not interesting countryside from the scenic point of view, but it is the home of the most beautiful wines imaginable, the great Médocs. It is the country of châteaux with world-renowned names: Margaux, Mouton-Rothschild, Latour, Beychevelle, Lafite, Cantemerle; magnificent seventeenth-century palaces, strange ungainly villas, stately nineteenth-century residences, castles that have been built and rebuilt and altered over seven hundred years – all of these can be found here; but it is not the houses that are important but their cellars. In the big Médoc cellars, as impressive as cathedrals in the half light, the wine matures in the small casks of the district, standing in long rows.

Médoc is a country of red wine – although a few estates, such as Château Margaux, make a little white wine as a curiosity – very great wines, wines of distinction, wines of a good middle class, and ordinary wines. It is divided into Médoc (formerly called Bas-Médoc) in the north, which produces ordinary to fair wines, and Haut-Médoc in the south, home of all the best growths. Three varieties of grape are used for Médoc wines, in proportions that can vary from year to year depending on weather conditions: Cabernet Sauvignon, which gives the wine its nobility and finesse; Merlot, which contributes roundness and fragrance; and Malbec which endows it with grace and lightness.

Médoc wines are always a little 'difficult'; they are, as it were, reserved, not revealing themselves at first. They have to be allowed time to mature, especially those of the highest quality. A great Médoc should not be drunk before it is at least five years old. Médocs have to be lovingly tended – no other wine is as sensitive to temperature. But once anyone has become acquainted with the nobility, the distinction, elegance and infinite

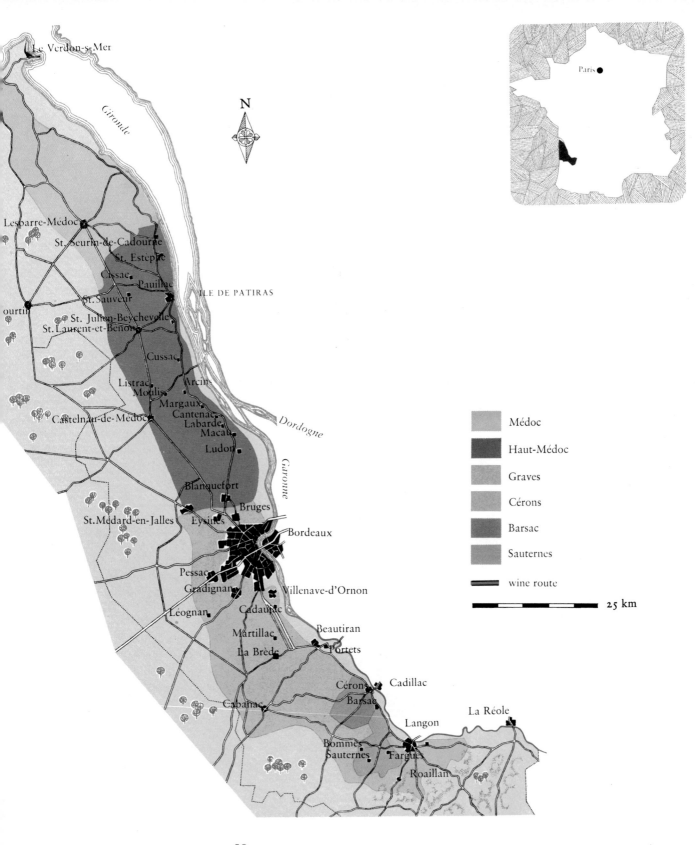

Le Verdon-s-Mer

Gironde

N

ÎLE DE PATIRAS

Lesparre-Médoc

St. Seurin-de-Cadourne

St. Estèphe

Cissac

Pauillac

St. Sauveur

ourtin

St. Julien-Beychevelle

St. Laurent-et-Benon

Cussac

Listrac

Moulis

Arcins

Margaux

Cantenac

Castelnau-de-Médoc

Labarde

Macau

Ludon

Dordogne

Garonne

Blanquefort

Bruges

St. Médard-en-Jalles

Eysines

Bordeaux

Pessac

Gradignan

Villenave-d'Ornon

Léognan

Cadaujac

Martillac

Beautiran

La Brède

Portets

Cérons

Cadillac

Cabanac

Barsac

La Réole

Langon

Bommes

Sauternes

Fargues

Roaillan

	Médoc
	Haut-Médoc
	Graves
	Cérons
	Barsac
	Sauternes
	wine route

25 km

Paris

59

subtlety characteristic of fine, mature Médocs, he will keep on returning to them all his life.

The wines gradually change in character from north to south. Those from the southerly Médoc communes – Macau, Cantenac, Margaux – are the lightest and most delicate; those from the communes of Listrac, St-Julien and Pauillac to the north have less subtle refinement but in its place gain more body. Further north still, in St-Estèphe, the wines have a masculine robustness and mettle.

GRAVES

This district, which derives its name from the white gravels abounding there, starts immediately outside the city of Bordeaux. It is flat country smelling of conifer woods in the warm summer sun. The Greek writer Plutarch already knew of the suitability of such country: 'Where pines grow the vine gives good wine.'

People in the importing countries tend to think of Graves as chiefly white wines, pale gold in colour, usually rather sweet and easily drinkable; sometimes they have been written off disparagingly as 'ladies' wines'. This is unfair to the wines of the Graves, quite apart from the fact that ladies today are as likely to be knowledgeable about wines as men.

60

This district certainly produces many ordinary white wines – the term Graves Supérieures signifies only that the wine has an alcoholic strength above 12% and is no indication of quality – but it also has many important white wines and even more splendid reds. One of the greatest red wines of Bordeaux, a *grand premier cru*, is a Graves red, Château Haut-Brion. A red Graves is a rather easier wine to get to know than a Médoc, less reserved as it were, and the good quality ones achieve a satin smoothness after no more than a few years' maturation. They are marvellous wines for a congenial evening with friends, for drinking with a creamy, not too sharp-tasting cheese. The best red Graves come from the communes of Léognan, Pessac, Martillac and Portets.

A remarkable feature here – and it occurs practically nowhere else – is that the same communes that produce great red wines can also grow excellent white ones. Although it is the semi-dry (*demi-sec*) white Graves that have proved particularly popular as exports, white Graves as drunk in Bordeaux can be so dry that they are served with oysters from the bay of Arcachon. But the dry Graves too have a pleasant soft quality and a delicate bouquet, yet with a hint of robustness that makes you think of warm gravel in the sun. They are delicious wines for serving with white seafish cooked with liberal amounts of butter.

SAUTERNES

Further south, still on the left bank of the Gironde, lies the little district of Sauternes, with gently rolling hills where the church spires of Sauternes itself, Bommes and Barsac rise out of the green. This is the country of the golden Sauvignon and Sémillon grapes, which hang from the vines in October among leaves that are beginning to turn; the fruit is ripe and full of juice, but it remains unpicked.

The grower looks at the sky and hopes fervently that October will stay fair, with a little cool mist in the mornings and a soft, caressing late year's sun in the afternoons. For this

Château d'Yquem

means that an ash-grey mould will appear on the grapes, the *Botrytis cinerea*. The fruit loses its golden colour, takes on a reddish tinge, then fades to a greyish beige. The skins, thin as membranes, burst, the water evaporates in the afternoon sun, and the grapes shrivel to wrinkled lumps.

Each morning the pickers go along the rows of vines with shears and baskets, plucking only completely dried grapes that have been visited by this beneficial rot, the *pourriture noble* as it is termed in French. This little harvest is pressed each evening.

This must, after a prolonged fermentation and due time for maturation in cask and bottle, will give the amber-coloured, sweet wines that the French call the 'exaggeration of the exquisite' and are the glory of Sauternes. Unique wines and, alas, very expensive ones. They cannot be other than costly. The risks are great: a heavy shower of rain in October when the overripe grapes are still on the vines brings a damaging mould in its train and the crop is lost. Harvesting is very labour intensive, because every morning, sometimes for as long as four weeks, it is only the rotted grapes that are picked. The yield is small: a dried and shrivelled grape produces only half as much juice as a normal ripe grape.

The very best Sauternes, and perhaps the finest white wine in the world, is that of Château d'Yquem, which stands on a hill and looks out in all its medieval sturdiness over a skein of châteaux at its feet. The Marquis de Lur-Saluces, an energetic owner of this château who died a few years ago, saw with sadness how his incomparable white wine, unforgettably sweet and the favourite once of tsars, emperors and kings, fell victim to a change in taste after World War II. He took up the struggle against the prevailing custom of only drinking Sauternes with a sweet dessert. In his opinion this luxurious wine should be drunk with a good pâté. This may sound unorthodox, but it should certainly be tried. (It does not have to be the forbiddingly expensive Château d'Yquem – there are other good Sauternes.) To fill your mouth with the rich taste of a fine pâté and taste the sweet spiciness of a Sauternes at the same time is to experience a rare enjoyment; and you will wholeheartedly concede that the marquis was right.

(The term Haut-Sauternes means nothing at all; when buying a Sauternes, make sure that the label bears the name of the commune – Sauternes, Barsac, Bommes, Preignac or Fargues.)

Bordeaux : Southeast

ENTRE-DEUX-MERS

The name Entre-deux-Mers suggests that this elongated wine district lies between two seas. This is not the case, however, for it is situated between two rivers, the Garonne and the Dordogne. It is a lovely piece of country with long rolling hills and small châteaux among the dark green of chestnut trees. The long, straight rows of vines follow the gentle undulations of the hills and often the whimsical grace of old appletrees holds the corners of the vineyards.

For ages past the golden grapes of the Garonne and Dordogne riversides have grown here, the Sémillon and Sauvignon which turn to a pinkish hue in the last stage of ripeness. The small growers of this area for long years made a sweet wine that seemed at first acquaintance to have something of the character of a simple Sauternes. However, as general taste turned increasingly to ever drier wines in the postwar years, and it became more and more difficult to sell sweet white Bordeaux, the progressive growers of this district decided, in a drastic change of course in 1955, henceforth to make dry white wines from their grapes. There are still conservative growers who let their grapes become overripe on the vines and make sweet wines from them, but in general an Entre-deux-Mers of today is a dry white wine containing a maximum of 3 grammes of grape sugar per litre. Typically it is a pleasant, light wine, but not one of the first rank. Entre-deux-Mers wines of the dryness favoured in Bordeaux are usually less popular in the importing countries than those with a less astringent quality. In Bordeaux they are drunk so dry because wines of this sort form an excellent accompaniment to the Arcachon oysters which are still eaten in the traditional manner here: hot, well-seasoned sausages alternate with mildly salty oysters and swigs of Entre-deux-Mers. Because of its low sugar content an Entre-deux-Mers wine would be difficult to keep without its addition of sulphur dioxide. For this reason letting the bottle stand open for twenty minutes before use is much to be recommended.

CÔTES DE BORDEAUX

Along the right bank of the Garonne, starting directly south of Bordeaux, runs a low, narrow ridge, the Côtes de Bordeaux. Red wines are grown in the northern part of this ridge and white in the south. They are labelled 'Premières Côtes de Bordeaux', often with the name of a commune added.

Red Côtes de Bordeaux wines are extremely agreeable; they are not expensive, they do not have to live up to the reputation of a great Médoc or a St-Emilion, but they have a good deal to offer for their moderate prices. They are a beautiful clear red in colour (in the Middle Ages the French termed this *clairet* and this is the origin of the English word claret, the generic name for red Bordeaux), they develop quickly and although simple they are amiably well balanced and never harsh.

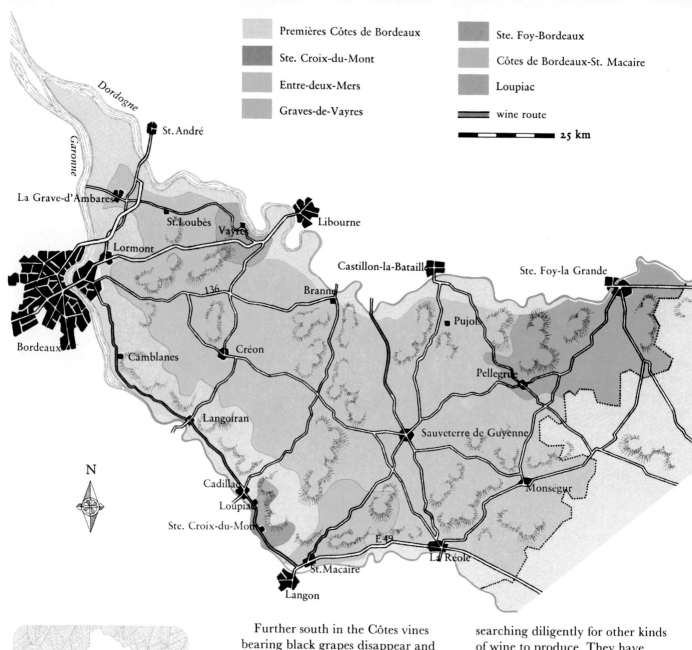

Premières Côtes de Bordeaux

Ste. Croix-du-Mont

Entre-deux-Mers

Graves-de-Vayres

Ste. Foy-Bordeaux

Côtes de Bordeaux-St. Macaire

Loupiac

wine route

25 km

Dordogne

Garonne

St. André

La Grave-d'Ambares

St. Loubès

Vayres

Libourne

Lormont

Castillon-la-Bataille

Ste. Foy-la Grande

Bordeaux

136

Branne

Pujols

Camblanes

Créon

Pellegrue

Langoiran

Sauveterre de Guyenne

Cadillac

Monségur

Loupiac

Ste. Croix-du-Mont

E 49

La Réole

St. Macaire

Langon

N

Paris

Further south in the Côtes vines bearing black grapes disappear and are replaced by the traditional whites, the Sémillon and Sauvignon. This too is a district of sweet white wines of outstanding quality – especially those of Ste-Croix-du-Mont and Loupiac – but commercially they have been rather pushed into the background. Sweet white wines are out of fashion. The growers in this southern part of the Côtes are searching diligently for other kinds of wine to produce. They have experimented with dry white wines; here and there vineyards have been planted for red wines. But unfortunately the soil and climate of the ridge seem to have been created just for the type of sweet white wine that has now become impossible to sell. All attempts to produce some other kind of wine of equal quality have so far been unsuccessful.

Bordeaux : Northeast

A steep, rocky hill rises out of the flat land along the right bank of the Dordogne and on it stands the small, ancient town of St-Emilion. In the fourth century AD, when France was still a prosperous province of the Roman empire, Ausonius, who was at one time a governor of the province, and later a consul, is said to have

CHATEAU
PETIT FAURIE DE SOUCHARD
GRAND CRU CLASSÉ
SAINT-ÉMILION
APPELLATION SAINT-ÉMILION GRAND CRU CLASSÉ CONTROLÉE

1967   *MAURICE JABIOL*
MISE EN BOUTEILLES   Propriétaire à SAINT-ÉMILION
AU CHATEAU   (GIRONDE)

1966
CHATEAU
YON LA TOUR FIGEAC
APPELLATION SAINT-ÉMILION CONTROLÉE

M. DUSSEAU · PROPRIÉTAIRE A SAINT-ÉMILION
10 - 12 Vol. Proc - Alc   HPA 043

been in the habit of retiring to a villa he owned here when the pressures of his native Burdigala (Bordeaux, already an important harbour) grew too much for him. In the summer he would work in his vineyard; in the winter he sat by the fire, drank his wine and wrote poems. There are some lines of his that run: 'The thrushes plunder the gleaming fruit of the vine, in the twilight the birdnets float like white clouds above the vineyard and in the morning they glisten with dew.' On the site where he is supposed to have tended his vines a stiff, nineteenth-century villa now stands, among vineyards where one of the greatest St-Emilions is grown – Château Ausone, named after the old Roman. In the subsequent confusions of the age of migrations the vineyards were destroyed or neglected. Then in the ninth century a hermit arrived from Brittany, withdrew to a cave in the hill to devote

his days to contemplation and caused a spring of clear water to well up. The spring still flows, but by an irony of fate, the saintly ascetic Aemilianus has given his name to a town famous for the luxuriousness of its wines. Followers of Aemilianus carved a church out of the solid rock of the hillside, the so-called Monolithic Church. Today it is used by the local equivalent of the Chevaliers du Tastevin, the Jurade, for their annual ceremonies when, dressed in their scarlet cloaks, they gather by torchlight to honour their wine. St-Emilion produces exclusively red wines; its citizens do not acknowledge the existence of white and the town is the only place in France where red wine is used for Holy Communion.

The steep, narrow streets of St-Emilion are paved with rough cobblestones, carried as ballast to the harbour of Libourne by the English wine fleet in the Middle Ages. The

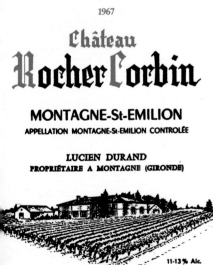

1967
Château
Rocher Corbin
MONTAGNE-St-EMILION
APPELLATION MONTAGNE-St-EMILION CONTROLÉE

LUCIEN DURAND
PROPRIÉTAIRE A MONTAGNE (GIRONDE)

11-13% Alc.

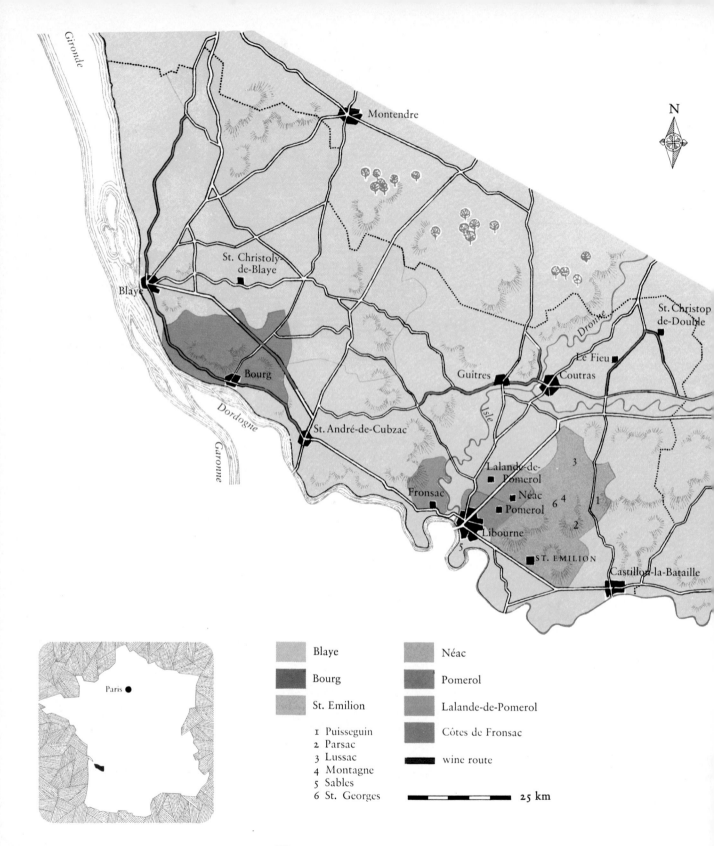

N

Gironde

Montendre

St. Christoly-
de-Blaye

Blaye

Droime

St. Christop
de-Double

Le Fieu

Guitres   Coutras

Bourg

Dordogne

St. André-de-Cubzac

Isle

Garonne

Lalande-de-
Pomerol
                 3
Fronsac   Néac   6 4   1
                 Pomerol
                         2
                 Libourne
            5
              ST. EMILION

Castillon-la-Bataille

Paris ●

	Blaye		Néac
	Bourg		Pomerol
	St. Emilion		Lalande-de-Pomerol

1 Puisseguin
2 Parsac
3 Lussac
4 Montagne
5 Sables
6 St. Georges

Côtes de Fronsac

wine route

25 km

coat of arms of the town still bears the leopards of the English monarchs Richard Lionheart and John Lackland, who inherited this lovely part of France from their mother, Eleanor of Aquitaine.

The wines of St-Emilion have a strong, masculine character. One of their great attractions is their mysterious, deep, glowing colour. They mostly have a rich bouquet and a luxurious taste that fills the mouth. When young they often have a slight bitterness to their aftertaste; in the best St-Emilions this develops with the years into their famous and characteristic flintiness of taste and aroma. St-Emilions develop more quickly than Médocs and remain at their peak for a long time. They must be given at least four years to mature, and they can reach twenty years and even more. They are wines that go with large helpings of meat, a generously proportioned entrecôte grilled on charcoal, or jugged hare. The best St-Emilions are Château Ausone and Château Cheval Blanc.

In the immediate vicinity of St-Emilion there are five communes entitled to their own appellations: St-Georges-St-Emilion, Montagne-St-Emilion, Lussac-St-Emilion, Puisseguin-St-Emilion and Sables-St-Emilion. They produce lesser wines than St-Emilion itself, but they have merit. They can mostly be drunk quite young and they include some very fair and robust wines.

POMEROL

North of St-Emilion, still on the right bank of the Dordogne, lies the little wine district of Pomerol with Lalande-de-Pomerol and Néac just to the east. Here too production is exclusively of red wines, almost as

The little town of St-Emilion

GRAND VIN

CHATEAU LARIVEAU

1966

CANON FRONSAC

APPELLATION CANON FRONSAC CONTRÔLÉE

11-13% ALC. GEH.   J. PUISERCUS, Propriétaire
                          à St-MICHEL-DE-FRONSAC (Gironde)

beautiful in colour as the St-Emilions. A Pomerol, however, is lighter in character and in this respect more like the Médocs. The soil of the vineyards here has a particularly high iron content and for this reason Pomerols are traditionally regarded as having medicinal properties. This iron content also gives the best Pomerols their remarkable scent; it has an earthy suggestion of truffles, those extravagant fungi from Périgord.

The wines of Lalande-de-Pomerol and Néac are rather sturdier, less elegant than the Pomerols, but they offer some agreeable drinking at reasonable prices. The best Pomerol is Château Pétrus.

FRONSAC

To the west, beside the Dordogne, there is another small red-wine district, comprising Côtes de Fronsac and Côtes Canon-Fronsac. Scenically this is one of the fairest parts of the Bordeaux region: rolling green countryside with beautiful distant views over vineyards, châteaux and the Dordogne.

The Fronsacs share the robustness characteristic of all the red wines of this region, attributable to the iron in the soil. Good Fronsacs often have

a spicy quality, especially the Canon-Fronsacs. They should not be drunk too young, because they are then rather harsh. Generally they are moderate in price, and more than worth it.

BOURG

The tiny fortified town of Bourg is situated in an attractive, gently undulating district beside the Dordogne, just before it joins the Garonne. Both white and red wines are grown here, but the reds are probably better known. These are quite sturdy wines, deep in colour and rich in bouquet: ideal table wines and ideal for cosy winter evenings with nuts and a piece of good farmhouse cheese. They should not be drunk too young: in their youth they are often harsh and inaccessible.

They mellow with the years, but remain very much wines for true lovers of Bordeaux who have learnt to appreciate their touch of underlying harshness.

BLAYE

The little fortress town of Blaye stands on the right bank of the Gironde, opposite Médoc and the narrow islands in midstream. White and red wines grow around Blaye. The whites are fruity, fragrant and dry wines drunk with caviar prepared locally from the roes of the sturgeon that still swim up the Gironde – unfortunately in small numbers. The red Blayais wines are generally rather mellower and 'easier' than those of Bourg and they can be drunk younger.

1res COTES   DE BLAYE

1961
CHATEAU MONCONSEIL
Appellation 1res Côtes de Blaye contrôlée
J.-P. BAUDET, propriétaire à PLASSAC (Gironde)

H.P.A: 043   ETIQ. DÉPOSÉE N° 170   10-12 Vol. Proc. Alc.

Cruse & Fils Frères
NÉGOCIANTS A BORDEAUX (GIRONDE)

1961
CHATEAU
COUBET
APPELLATION COTES DE BOURG CONTRÔLÉE

M. MIGNE, Propriétaire à Villeneuve-de-Blaye

PRODUCE OF CRUSE FRANCE

Loire

The Loire flows through the heart of France, the most French of all her rivers. From Auvergne it goes northwest through the old dukedom of Berry, a country golden with cornfields and green with vineyards, patterned by small rivers with weeping willows along their banks. The first really important vineyards on the Loire come at Pouilly-sur-Loire. This is a small village, just one long street, with less than two thousand inhabitants and – this could only happen in France – four restaurants with a Michelin star, one to every five hundred souls. To them people come from near and far every Sunday to eat salmon, pike and turbot. With the food they drink the wine of Pouilly, the Pouilly-Fumé, golden in colour with a tinge of green to it, fruity and just slightly spicy. Some people detect a faintly smoky taste and assert that this is the reason for the name *fumé*. Others allege that *fumé* refers to the pale grey, smoky film that appears on the Sauvignon grapes in September. Whatever the truth of the matter Pouilly-Fumé is a wine with a singular, enigmatic bouquet. Marie Antoinette was so fond of this wine that she had perfume distilled from the fragrant blossom of Pouilly vines.

SANCERRE

Further north the small fortified town of Sancerre stands on a hill on the opposite side of the Loire. At the foot of this hill, in a setting of luxuriant green, lie the little wine villages of Chavignol and Amigny. Mushroom-coloured goats frisk among the vines. Goat's milk cheeses mature on long wooden racks in the dairies, and wines in the cellars, the fruity,

The Loire in Anjou

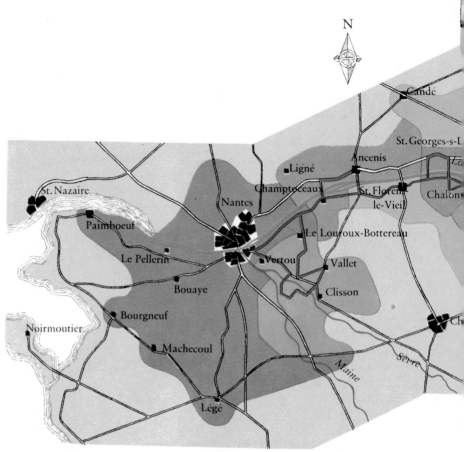

soft and at the same time refreshing
wines of Sancerre, greenish-yellow
in colour. And how splendid they taste
with those small white cheeses!
Sancerre is becoming increasingly
known and appreciated abroad as a
moderately priced wine. Its cool,
light and fruity quality can stimulate
the appetite in the manner of an
apéritif. A Sancerre is always drunk
young. It is ready for sale a few months
after the grape harvest and after three
or four years in the bottle it generally
loses its greatest charm, its freshness.

QUINCY AND REUILLY

Also in the upper Loire valley are the
small wine districts of Quincy and
Reuilly. They produce fresh-tasting
white wines; like Pouilly and Sancerre
they are made from the Sauvignon
grape, are drunk young, and are

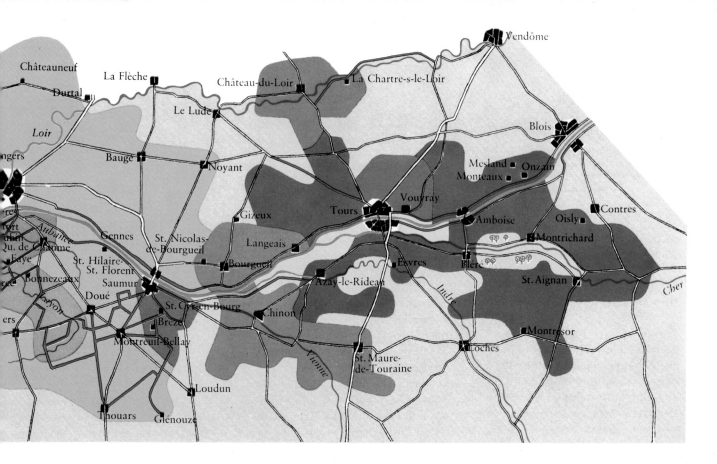

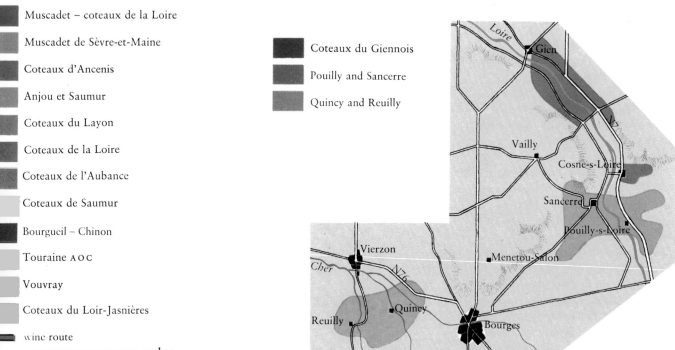

Muscadet – coteaux de la Loire

Muscadet de Sèvre-et-Maine

Coteaux d'Ancenis

Anjou et Saumur

Coteaux du Layon

Coteaux de la Loire

Coteaux de l'Aubance

Coteaux de Saumur

Bourgueil – Chinon

Touraine A O C

Vouvray

Coteaux du Loir-Jasnières

wine route

Coteaux du Giennois

Pouilly and Sancerre

Quincy and Reuilly

25 km

excellent with all kinds of freshwater fish, and of course goat's milk cheeses.

TOURAINE

Travelling further downstream beneath wide skies and past the magnificent châteaux built by French kings for their queens and favourites, we come to the lovely countryside of Touraine where, according to tradition, vines flourished before the Romans came to Gaul. This is also the country of St Martin, whose ass browsed on the vines and gave growers the idea of annual pruning (donkeys still go by the name of Martin in Touraine). St Martin is also said to have introduced the principal local vine, the Pineau de Loire, from his native Hungary. The wines of Touraine were drunk by the French court in the great salons of the châteaux, under carved and gilded ceilings, in Chinon, Amboise, Blois and Chambord. And these wines inspired two of France's greatest poets, Ronsard and Rabelais, who were born in the Loire country.

The best-known wine of Touraine is Vouvray from the village of the same name on the right bank. The grapes for it are picked late, when they are overripe and extremely sweet. The resulting wine can therefore have a high alcohol content, sometimes

approaching 14% – but this is barely noticeable because Vouvray is soft and fruity, with the taste of the grape and the delicate aroma of quinces. 'How good is God to give us this wonderful wine. By my soul, it is a silken wine!', wrote Rabelais of Vouvray. Vouvrays can be drunk young, but a really good one can live to a tremendous age. There are growers here and there with Vouvrays a century old in their cellars which they allow favoured guests to sample. Sparkling wine is made from Vouvray in the limestone caves along the Loire in the classical manner of Champagne, and so is some enchanting *pétillant* or slightly sparkling wine. Twenty miles further downstream there are two villages, Chinon on the left bank and Bourgueil on the right, which produce red wine, a rarity in the Loire. Bourgueil is an attractive wine, fruity with a delightful scent

of ripe raspberries. It can be drunk young, but patience is always rewarded with a Bourgueil; with age – and they can attain at least twenty years – they acquire a fine, elegant roundness.

ANJOU AND SAUMUR

Westwards down the Loire, broad and mighty here, but shallow and full of sandbanks, the little town of Saumur stands on the left bank with its splendid medieval castle high on a hill, and to the west again is the lovely countryside of Anjou. Big, full white wines are grown here and they are headier than might be thought – Louis XI once called them 'drops of gold'.

The sweet white wines of the Côteaux du Layon are renowned. Like Sauternes they are made from grapes affected by *pourriture noble*.

SAUMUR

APPELLATION SAUMUR CONTROLÉE

ALBERT BESOMBES, S.A. NÉGOCIANT-ÉLEVEUR A ST HILAIRE-ST FLORENT. FRANCE

Saumur also produces plain, quite dry wines, agreeable sparkling wines, and fresh pleasant rosés.

Anjou is best known for its rosés, many of which are cheap and unpretentious everyday wines and especially suited to summer evenings. For those who want something a little better there is the Rosé de Cabernet, made as the name suggests from the Cabernet grape. Anjou rosés have become so popular that they are tending more and more to supplant the whites, which is a pity for there are some very good white Anjous, such as the famed Coulée de Serrant.

In the seventeenth and eighteenth centuries the whole wine trade in Anjou was in the hands of Dutch merchants who had their offices and cellars along the Loire. They bought up the best qualities and left the cheaper sorts for Paris.

MUSCADET

It seems as if the vine is loath ever to take leave of the Loire, for the last vineyards occur just before the river flows into the sea below Nantes. These are the Muscadet vineyards – a confusing name. It is not the name of a village or district but of a vine, and it has nothing to do with the muscat grape, as is sometimes

supposed. The Muscadet is a vine of Burgundian origin that was not planted in this green, moist country until about 1700. Muscadet is a remarkable wine, very light, almost as clear as water, with a low alcohol content, and it is very dry. It often has a slightly salt aftertaste. This is due to microscopic salt crystals blown onto the grapes by the sea winds from Brittany. Muscadet is bottled young, usually a few months after vintage. Sometimes there are barely perceptible carbon dioxide bubbles in the wine, the result of a slight secondary fermentation in the bottle. The best Muscadet is *sur lie*, literally 'on the lees': the wine is drawn directly from its first cask without any intervening transference to a second, and without filtering, so that some deposit remains in the wine. The less a Muscadet comes into contact with the air the better, and lighter, it will be. In Brittany Muscadet is the wine for drinking with oysters, mussels, crab, all types of shellfish in fact, and is altogether excellent with fish. On hot days a glass of slightly chilled Muscadet is as fresh as a sea wind in April.

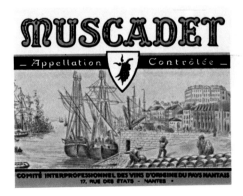

When buying Muscadet look for the words 'Muscadet de Sèvre et Maine' on the label for this gives some guarantee of quality.

Alsace

Alsace lies between the Rhine and the Vosges, its rear protected from the damp and chilly west winds, its face towards the east and the morning sun, the best sun for vineyards. The Alsace wine district is long and narrow, running from north to south, lapping the first slopes of the Vosges and into the Rhine valley. It is dotted with small, picturesque wine towns and villages with black-and-white, half-timbered houses, clock towers and fountains where geraniums bloom in pink and red abundance. Alsace is one of the friendliest and most beautiful winelands of Europe, and also one of the oldest in France. When the Romans built a military camp at the spot where four of their roads met, the present Strasbourg (the Dutch still call it Straatsburg, which shows the origin of the name), the vines were already climbing the green slopes of the hills. When Charlemagne established the first great western European empire, Alsace already had 800 wine villages; and when at the Treaty of Verdun his realm was divided among his three grandsons, the boundaries of the middle portion allotted to Lotharius were drawn to include Alsace so that it could supply him with wine. Alsace is a transitional zone between France and Germany. This can be seen in its towns and villages, heard in the language, and, above all, tasted in the local cuisine which combines solid German qualities with French refinement. Alsatian wines have something of the German Rhineland about them but also a typically French grace and lightness. Goethe once remarked that in Alsace French yeast had leavened the somewhat heavy German dough.

The wines of Alsace are white – some red and rosé is made in the north around Rosheim, but it is of little importance. The greatest charm of the region's wines is their purity and naturalness. 'Between us and the vine there is only the Good Lord' they say in Alsace. The wine is everywhere made in the old traditional manner; it stays in the cask for several months, it is transferred to clean casks and duly bottled. And this is the secret of its characteristic fruitiness. In every Alsace wine you can taste the

Alsace, transitional zone between France and Germany

grape. It is altogether reasonable, therefore, that Alsace wines are named not after their place of origin, like practically all other French wines, but after their grape variety.

Some eight different kinds of grapes grow in the vineyards of Alsace: two 'peasant' types, the Chasselas and Knipperlé, two of rather greater prestige, the Sylvaner and the Pinot Blanc, and four superior grapes, the Riesling, Gewürztraminer, Muscat and Tokay. The everyday tap wines, which the Alsatians drink in unimaginable quantities in pleasant little taverns behind Strasbourg Cathedral, in the narrow medieval streets of Colmar and in all the winemaking towns and villages, are made from the Chasselas and Knipperlé varieties plus one of the better ones. This type of wine is called Zwicker; it is fresh, young and has the engaging property of quenching thirst, but happily never completely.

Edelzwicker is made from a blend of superior grapes; this is the carafe wine served in most of the small restaurants of Alsace. However, the real nature of Alsace wines is best discovered by tasting the typical unmixed wines that preserve the character of the grape.

Sylvaner   Light and dry, with a gentle bouquet that is more pervasive than might be thought: a few glasses of Sylvaner can fill a room with a fragrance of spring flowers. A Sylvaner is very suitable for summer apéritifs and with light hors d'oeuvres.
Pinot   Light and dry, without a very distinctive bouquet, but possessing the enchanting freshness of a spring morning.
Riesling   The best of all: it is called the 'king of Alsace wines', dry, robust and masculine, with the sometimes staggeringly beautiful Riesling bouquet. In Alsace it is drunk with the famous local sauerkraut; it also goes excellently with fish, and with chicken or veal in a creamy white sauce there is perhaps nothing better.
Muscat   Very dry, with the full, spicy bouquet of its kind. It can be drunk with a well-flavoured cheese and also goes surprisingly well with a pâté.
Tokay   Very fine and fragrant, slightly spicy, sturdy; a wine with

75

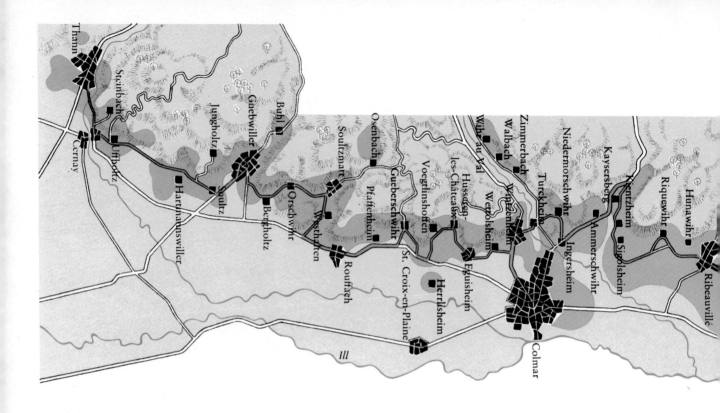

more depth than might be suspected at first taste. It can be even drunk with game. It is a particularly good partner for cheese and pâté. Tokay often has a subtle hint of pink in its golden colour.

Gewürztraminer The heaviest, and headiest, of the wines of Alsace, with a strong, markedly spicy bouquet. It is dry, but at the same time gives an impression of rounded richness. A Gewürztraminer can even be drunk

with the stronger types of cheese, such as Roquefort, or Munster from the Vosges (in Alsace they serve this with a bowl of caraway or cummin seeds to dip the cheese in – it is worth trying a Gewürztraminer with a cummin-flavoured cheese, Dutch Leiden for instance).

Alsace wines are drunk young, but this does not mean that they cannot age. A few years ago a bricked-up

recess was uncovered in a wine cellar in Riquewihr. In it were found a large number of bottles of wine dating from the last century. These were officially sampled in the presence of the local *chevaliers*, the Confrérie de Saint-Etienne, and an invited group of foreign wine journalists. The wine was still excellent, even one of 1848.

Each of the grape varieties grown in this wine region has its particular favoured area. The Sylvaner does

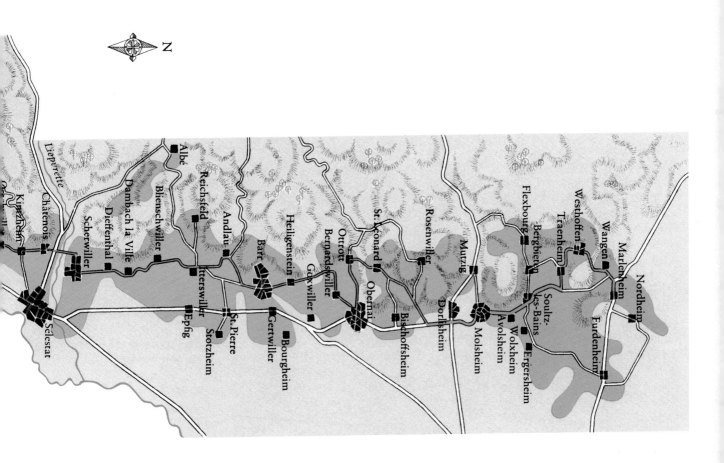

N

Lièpvrette

Kintzheim
Châtenois
Scherwiller
Dieffenthal
Dambach la Ville
Blienschwiller
Albé
Reichsfeld
Itterswiller
Epfig
Storzheim
St. Pierre
Andlau
Barr
Gertwiller
Heiligenstein
Bourgheim
Goxwiller
Bernardswiller
Ottrott
St. Léonard
Obernai
Bischoffsheim
Rosenwiller
Dorlisheim
Murzig
Molsheim
Avolsheim
Wolxheim
Soultz-les-Bains
Ergersheim
Flexbourg
Bergbieten
Traenheim
Westhoffen
Wangen
Marlenheim
Nordheim
Furdenheim

Sélestat

best in the north, around Barr; the Riesling flourishes in the neighbourhood of Riquewihr and Ribeauville, and so does the Muscat; good Gewürztraminers come from Riquewihr and Turckheim.

In the seventeenth and eighteenth centuries Alsace wines were shipped down the Rhine in vast quantities and many rummers of 'Rhenish' quaffed in paintings, books and plays of the period probably contained wine from Alsace. In the years between 1870 and 1918 when Alsace was German it was again the fate of Alsace wines to remain an anonymous component of Rhineland and Moselle exports. After 1918, however, the people of Alsace, inspired by pride in the fact that they were once more French, approached their wine industry with a new *élan*. Since World War II their wine has had an assured and unique place among French wines of quality.

Paris

Champagne

Millions of years ago the sea surged where now the green hills of Champagne roll towards the horizon. Year after year, and century after century, millions of shellfish lived and died in this sea and a thick layer of chalk was gradually built up from the shells that sank to the bottom. The sea receded and movements in the earth's crust thrust up this layer of chalk to form the hills of the old *comté* of Champagne. The Romans knew that this chalk was good for white wines, for they started vineyards here. In this cool, soft climate excellent light, fragrant white wines were made which in spring produced streamers of carbon dioxide bubbles. When the French kings went to Reims to be anointed by the archbishop in the cathedral, wine from this district was served at the coronation banquet. In those days it was still wine, not the festive, sparkling champagne we know today.

By tradition it was the cellarmaster of the abbey of Hautvillers, Dom Pérignon, who in the second half of the seventeenth century discovered the secret of the bubbles and learned to make use of it. He was particularly intrigued by the fact that his young white wine underwent a second fermentation in the spring, and reports reached him from England that it became so unsettled in cellars that corks flew out of the bottles. Dom Pérignon began to experiment and discovered the principle of secondary fermentation in the bottle (see page 24f). He also found out that the best champagne is made when wine from white Chardonnay grapes is blended with wine from black Pinot Noir.

A solution then had to be found to the problem of the deposit that formed in the bottle during the second fermentation. The method evolved consisted of upending the bottles so that the sediment settled on the cork. The cork was then removed, taking the deposit with it, and a new cork was quickly and deftly inserted. Today in the big cellar-wineries, the *maisons* as they are called, of Reims, Epernay and Ay you can see the bottles upside down on long wooden racks, the *pupitres*. They are turned each day so that the deposit slips to the bottom and builds up against the cork. The neck of the bottle is put in a freezing mixture, the plug of sediment freezes

Champagne vineyards beside the Marne

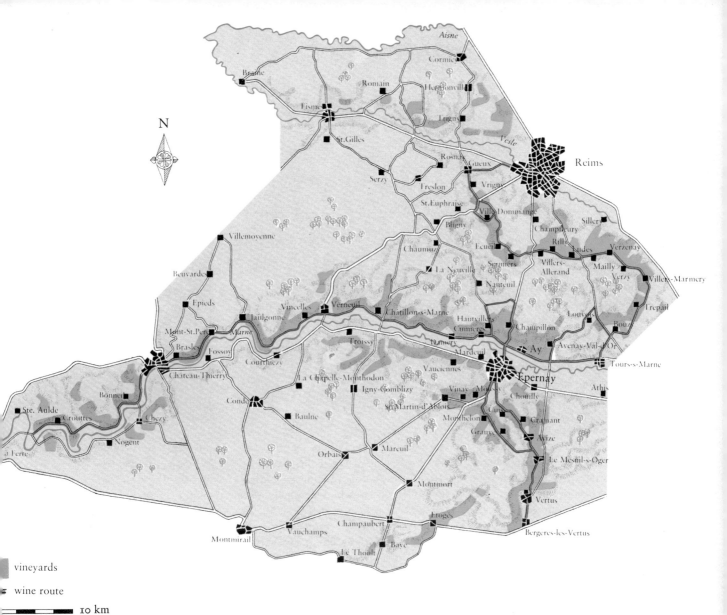

N

Paris

vineyards

wine route

├──────────┤ 10 km

to the cork which is then removed (less wine is lost in this way than by the earlier technique). At the same time as this is being done, the *dosage* is added. This is a solution of cane sugar in old wine which gives champagne the required degree of sweetness. All champagne is naturally dry. If no more than a half per cent of sugar is added then it remains dry: *champagne brut*, which is regarded as the best quality. For *champagne sec* 2 to 3

per cent sugar is added; for the *demi-sec* 7 to 10 per cent. Most champagne consists of not only a mixture of wine from black and white grapes (except *blanc de blancs*, made exclusively from white), but also of a blend of grapes from different years. Only in exceptionally good years is there a vintage champagne, i.e. one made entirely from grapes of one year: this is *champagne millésimé*, which is always *brut*.

79

Côtes du Rhône

When adventurous Greeks from Phocis sailed into the marshy delta of the Rhône in 600 BC and founded the port of Massilia (Marseille), they brought the vine with them. Descendants of this parent vine, the Viognier, still grow along the banks of the Rhône from Marseille to just below Lyon. The Rhône vineyards cover an extensive area: no fewer than 138 communes produce the wine entitled to the appellation 'Côtes du Rhône', in the north of the region from Vienne to Valence, and in the south from Orange to Avignon where the wine-growing area bulges towards the east. Many decent, unpretentious wines are grown here, almost exclusively red, robust, spicy in scent. You can drink them young, and cold, and they go with the spiciest dishes, with garlic and piquant sauces. Generally they offer good value for their modest price. However, there are also a number of wines of

Châteauneuf-du-Pape

considerable quality here – and even the rarest wine of France, Château Grillet, from a vineyard near Condrieu of only five acres which produces about ten casks of wine a year. It can be sampled in only two restaurants in France: at Madame Point's in Vienne and at Beau Rivage in Condrieu. The most famous wine of the Côtes du Rhône is Châteauneuf-du-Pape which grows north of Avignon near the village of the same name. In the

thirteenth century life was so unsettled in Rome, and wine so often poisoned, that the Pope and his cardinals sought the greater security offered by Avignon, where a mighty castle was soon built for the Pope. Because even popes needed relaxation and a change of scene, a new castle (the *château neuf*) was constructed among the hills four miles up the valley. The vineyards here were started by certain popes with an interest in

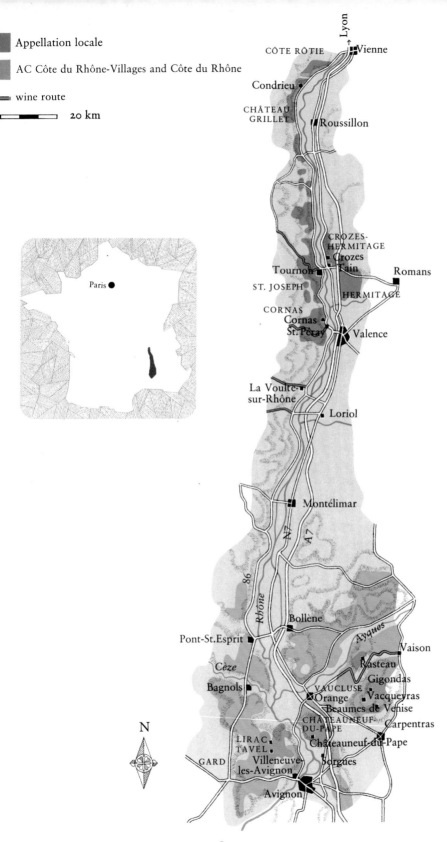

Lyon

Vienne

CÔTE RÔTIE

Condrieu

CHÂTEAU GRILLET

Roussillon

CROZES-HERMITAGE

Crozes

Tain

Tournon

Romans

ST. JOSEPH

HERMITAGE

CORNAS

Cornas

St. Péray

Valence

La Voulte-sur-Rhône

Loriol

Montélimar

N7

A7

86

Rhône

Bollène

Ayques

Pont-St.Esprit

Vaison

Cèze

Rasteau

Gigondas

Bagnols

VAUCLUSE

Orange

Vacqueyras

Beaumes de Venise

Carpentras

CHÂTEAUNEUF-DU-PAPE

Châteauneuf-du-Pape

LIRAC

TAVEL

Sorgues

GARD

Villeneuve-les-Avignon

Avignon

N

Paris

viticulture, hence the name. The vines grow among large boulders brought down in prehistoric times by the river Rhône. During the day they absorb the heat of the sun and at night they radiate it to the benefit of the surrounding vines. This is said to be the secret of the deep glow and fire of the wines of Châteauneuf.

Less renowned, but worth getting to know, are the spicy, amethyst-red wines and the fragrant, golden whites of Hermitage and its hinterland of Crozes Hermitage. Particularly agreeable, robust and fragrant red wines are grown round the village of Gigondas, where William of Orange owned vineyards.

The premier Rhône wine, however, is Côte Rôtie, dark red in colour, potent and with a distinctive bouquet. It is at the height of its development after three or four years.

The pleasantest rosés in the whole of France come from the bank of the Rhône opposite Avignon, from Tavel and Lirac, wines as warm and tender as the kiss of a Provençale girl, or so they say in Avignon.

GRAND CRU

Domaine de Longval
TAVEL
APPELLATION TAVEL CONTROLÉE
GEORGES BERNARD PROPRIÉTAIRE A TAVEL (GARD)

Chablis

The Basse-Bourgogne between Auxerre and Tonnerre is a rather remote area. It does not have the resplendent tourist attractions of the Côte d'Or, no world-famous restaurants, no Romanesque churches and abbeys. It is a quiet, green farming country with gently undulating contours. In this small, peaceful, forgotten district there nevertheless grows one of the best of the white Burgundies, Chablis. The vineyards are on chalk formed originally by countless millions of oyster shells, the detritus of the sea that once covered this region. Is it perhaps this history that has made Chablis the ideal wine for oysters?

In the seventeenth century when large quantities of oysters were eaten, and for one person to consume dozens at a sitting was not thought at all unusual, Chablis became the favourite wine to wash them down with. In some countries it even became

known as 'oyster water'. Samuel Pepys, whose diary is such an inexhaustible source of information on everyday life in the seventeenth century, reported that he kept Chablis in his cellar to drink with oysters.

Chablis is not only a good accompaniment to oysters, but will partner any fine fish, trout or sole, salmon or turbot.

Chablis is a delicate wine made from the white Chardonnay grape. It is greenish-gold in colour, bone dry, softly fragrant and yet with more strength and depth than might initially be supposed.

Often the best Chablis wines are produced in years that are too cold and damp for other Burgundies. It is when the grapes are picked before they are quite ripe that Chablis is produced with the delicacy and freshness that are its chief charm.

The best Chablis comes from the immediate environs of the little town

of that name and it is labelled with the name of its vineyard, for example Vaudésir, Grenouilles, Preuses, and the classification Chablis *grand cru*. The next best category is Chablis *premier cru*, usually with the name of the vineyard. After this comes Chablis, then Petit Chablis which is grown not on the chalk but on a mixture of chalk and clay. Petit Chablis is lower in alcoholic strength than the other Chablis and lacks their finesse.

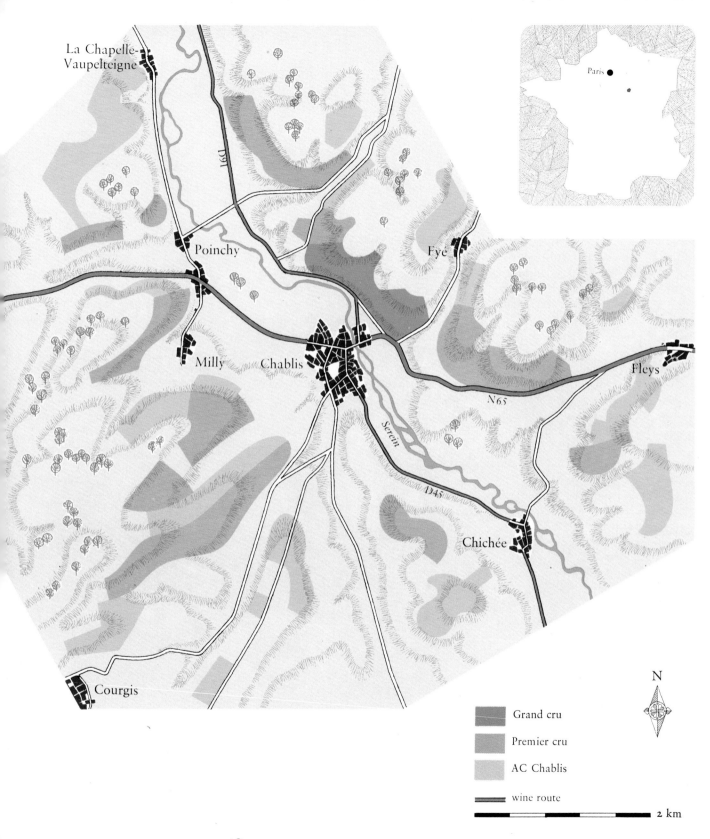

La Chapelle-
Vaupelteigne

Poinchy

Fyé

Milly

Chablis

Fleys

N65

Serein

D45

Chichée

Courgis

Paris

Grand cru

Premier cru

AC Chablis

wine route

N

2 km

Côte d'Or

The sloping ground known as the Côte d'Or is a long narrow strip, more than twenty-five miles long from north to south and only about two and a half miles wide, to the west of Route Nationale 6. In October, when the vines turn gold, bronze and vermilion, it looks like a vast length of brocade spread under the autumn sun. This, however, is not the explanation of the name: *or* here apparently does not mean 'gold' but is a shortened form of *orient*. Prosaically enough, the Côte d'Or is the east-facing slope. Its northern part is called the Côte de Nuits, the southern part, beginning at Aloxe-Corton, the Côte de Beaune. It is a country of vineyards, of small, ancient wine villages, of stoutly built abbeys, of occasional small châteaux – and also of the beautiful town of Beaune with the fifteenth-century Hospice, the Hôtel-Dieu, at its centre; this has remained a home for the sick and aged ever since it was donated to the town by Nicolas Rolin, chancellor to Philip the Good, Duke of Burgundy. The courtyard has for many long years been the traditional site of the annual auction of wines from the Hospice vineyards, held on the third Sunday in November. Ever since the fifteenth century the proceeds from these sales have been used for the care of those who seek shelter or healing at the Hôtel-Dieu.
The vineyards of the Côte d'Or

are a mosaic no less complicated than the pattern of polychrome tiles on the roof of the Hospice. The French wine writer Raymond Dumay once called the Côte d'Or a work of art of the same order as the Acropolis or Chartres Cathedral. The vineyards have been built up with mathematical precision and an unerring feeling for what was the best possible siting. The siting of the *climats*, as vineyards are called in Burgundy, within the available area

is right to within a couple of feet for ensuring the most favourable soil composition, height of ground, and situation with regard to the sun for producing the best possible wines. It should be noted too that most of these vineyards date from the early Middle Ages, many of them from before the year 1000, when people had no notion of biochemistry, soil analysis or meteorology, and that today the best wines still come from the vineyards

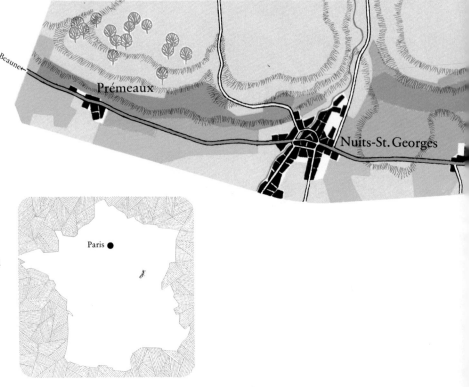

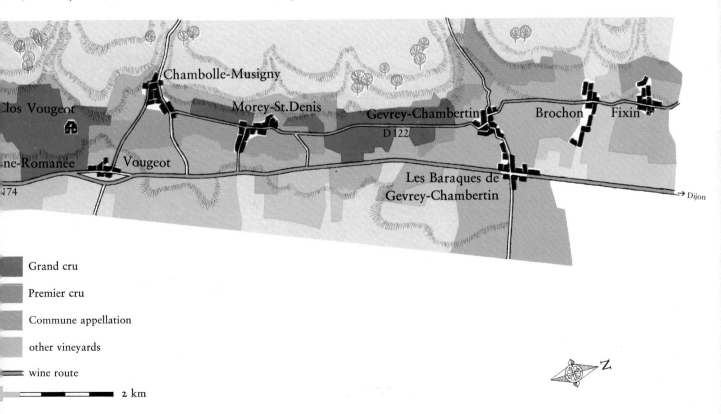

Joseph Drouhin

HOSPICES
DE BEAUNE

Meursault-Charmes
Appellation Contrôlée
Cuvée Albert Grivault
1964

ACQUÉREUR : JOSEPH DROUHIN A BEAUNE, COTE-D'OR

hat were marked out at that time. Many vineyards of the Côte were ormer monastic estates that were onfiscated and divided among small ine growers during the French Revolution. For this reason there are many small and even tiny holdings long the Côte which often together make up one famous vineyard. These mallholders can bestow great care n their vines and produce excellent ine, but they do not have the

facilities for nurturing their wine once made or of marketing it and so they sell it to wine dealers who undertake these aspects of the business. Unfortunately the very great Burgundies from these famous old vineyards have now become so expensive as to belong to legend: Chambertin, Napoleon's favourite wine, although wasted on him in the sense that he was no connoisseur; Romanée, prescribed for Louis XIV

by his physician – the king is supposed to have said that a disease for which such medicine had to be taken was a gift of heaven. These wines cannot be anything but costly for their vineyards are small (Musigny is 25 acres, Romanée less than 3 acres, Romanée-Conti 5 acres, Chambertin 69 acres) and the demand, especially in the United States, is great.

There are Burgundies slightly less prestigious than these legendary wines,

Grand cru

Premier cru

Commune appellation

other vineyards

wine route

2 km

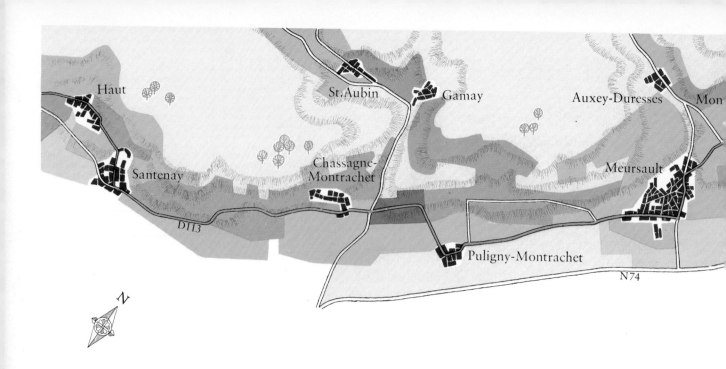

Haut

St. Aubin

Gamay

Auxey-Duresses

Mon

Santenay

Chassagne-
Montrachet

Meursault

D113

Puligny-Montrachet

N74

N

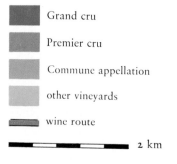

Grand cru

Premier cru

Commune appellation

other vineyards

wine route

2 km

Paris ●

86

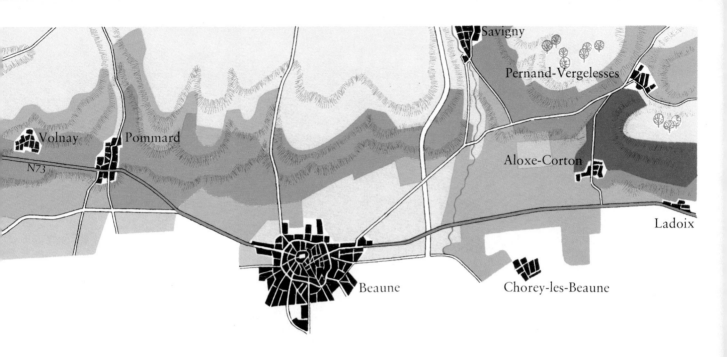

but still very good and also rather costly, which are sold under the name of their commune; examples are Beaune, Pommard, or Volnay. Many Côte de Nuits communes and a few of the Côte de Beaune have their own name coupled with that of the best-known vineyard within their boundaries, such as Gevrey-Chambertin, Vosne-Romanée, Aloxe-Corton, Chambolle-Musigny, and Puligny-Montrachet. Wines

labelled in this way do not come from the illustrious vineyard that follows the hyphen but from a number of other sites within the commune boundaries. But they are often beautiful wines, especially if they come from an old-established dealer.

Then there are villages which collectively are entitled to an appellation, the Côte de Beaune-Villages and the Côte de Nuits-Villages. Wines sold at the Hospice

auction are labelled Hospice de Beaune with in addition the name of the original donor of the vineyard – Nicolas Rolin for example.

All the wines of the Côte de Nuits are red, made from the Pinot Noir grape. The Côte de Beaune has red (Pinot Noir) and white (Chardonnay). There is a clearly defined difference between the wines of the two Côtes. Good Côte de Nuits wines are what most lovers of Burgundy would term

Unfortunately Montrachet comes from a small vineyard of scarcely 17 acres with a production of 100 hectolitres. It is therefore prohibitively expensive. Happily consolation can be found in Puligny-Montrachet, from the same commune, which is a particularly fine, aristocratic white wine. Besides the great Burgundies mentioned there are also less exalted ones. The red Bourgogne Passe-Tout-Grains is made from a mixture of Pinot and Gamay grapes and often comes from vineyards to the east of Route Nationale 6. Bourgogne Aligoté is a dry white Burgundy from the grape of the same name that lends itself particularly well to making Kir. This is a fresh-tasting apéritif of one part *crème de cassis* (blackcurrant liqueur) and three parts white Burgundy. It is named after Canon Kir, a great winelover who for many years was the revered mayor of Dijon.

real Burgundies: rich, sensual, robust, wines that fill the mouth, are silken smooth and have a rich, spicy bouquet that evokes woods and wild berries, sometimes cherries or, like the Vosne-Romanée, violets. They could be said to be wines of the expansive gesture. They should not be drunk too young; they need at least six years to mature.

The red wines of the Côte de Beaune are lighter, elegant and feminine, their bouquets are subtle and refined, but often with that spiciness characteristic of good Burgundies. They mature more quickly than Côte de Nuits. The wines of Savigny have a marvellous soft scent, those of Volnay are graceful and well balanced (Volnay was the favourite wine of the elegant and epicurean Louis XV); and Victor Hugo called Pommard 'an honest Burgundian'. It is an interesting fact that near Puligny-Montrachet, where predominantly

white wines are grown, there is a small acre of red, Chassagne-Montrachet, and even more remarkably these wines are more like Nuits wines in character than those of Beaune. Again it is a question of subsoil.

The white Burgundy vineyards begin past Pommard near the little town of Meursault (the Latin name, Muris Saltus, is supposed to mean that it lies a mouse's leap away from the red vineyards). Meursault is a beauty of a white wine, greenish gold with a flavour of ripe grapes and a bouquet that suggests hazelnuts. A remarkable thing about Meursault is that it is absolutely dry but conveys no sense of dryness to the tongue; and as it ages it becomes soft and mellow.

Further southwest lies the village of Puligny-Montrachet where the greatest white Burgundy grows; with Château d'Yquem in Bordeaux it is the greatest white wine of France.

PULIGNY-MONTRACHET

Clos de la Garenne

APPELLATION PULIGNY-MONTRACHET CONTRÔLÉE

DOMAINE
DU CHATEAU DE PULIGNY-MONTRACHET
ROLAND THÉVENIN, *propriétaire*

ALC. 12-14%

Mâconnais and Beaujolais

As you travel south from the Côte d'Or, towards the sun, the vine remains part of the background to your journey. South of Chagny, just west of RN 6, there is the pretty and undeservedly little-known district of Mercurey. Here grow moderately priced red wines that resemble the wines of the Côte de Beaune-Villages in character: with a spicy bouquet, they are soundly constituted and have a certain elegance. North of the village of Mercurey is Rully, where a decent white wine is grown with a natural tendency to secondary fermentation and from which excellent *vin mousseux* is therefore made; and to the south lies Givry, the home of not-too-well-known but good red wines. The south-bound traveller notices after a few miles how very gradually the atmosphere of the countryside changes, taking on something of the character of the Midi: the Burgundian style of tiled roof disappears and less steeply pitched roofs with orange-red *romaines*, the Roman pattern of tile, begin to be seen. It is a wide, green, peaceful countryside country. Then out of the green sea of vines two steep cliffs rise like the bows of gigantic ships. The more southerly of the two is the famed Solutré where in distant prehistoric times Palaeolithic hunters chased wild horses to the cliff top so that they plunged over, providing horsemeat for the taking down below. This is the region of the Mâconnais, taking its name from the town of Mâcon on the river Saône; it has been well called the 'valley of cellars'. It was the birthplace of the poet Lamartine who wrote: 'The vines sing as their riches are plucked, it seems as if the earth itself rejoices when the vintage is gathered in.' In October the whole landscape is a glorious sea of gold and bronze. In the seventeenth century the wines of Mâcon were still so little known that a grower from the district set off for Paris with two casks of the wine on his ox wagon to present them in person to Louis XIV, hoping in this way to make it known and liked at court. There is both red and white Mâcon. The red is a plain, straightforward wine, robust and well endowed with scent and flavour, and it can be drunk young – but it

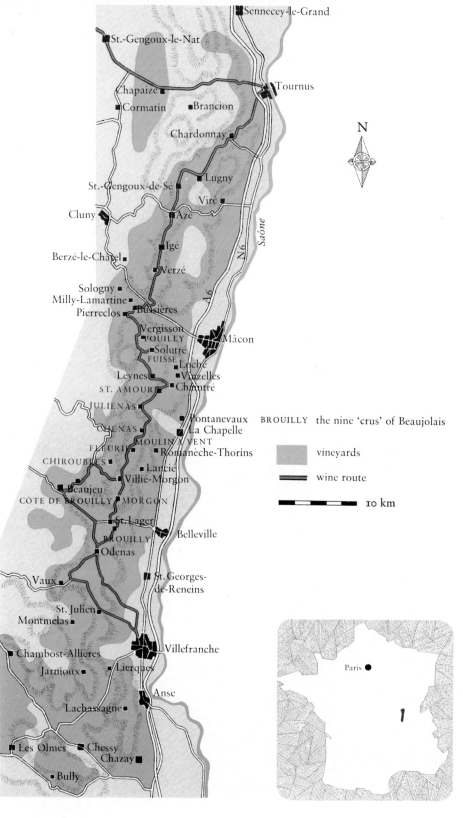

On map:
Sennecey-le-Grand
St.-Gengoux-le-Nat
Chapaize
Cormatin
Brancion
Tournus
Chardonnay
St.-Gengoux-de-Sé
Lugny
Viré
Cluny
Azé
Igé
Berzé-le-Châtel
Verzé
Sologny
Milly-Lamartine
Bussières
Pierreclos
Vergisson
POUILLY
Mâcon
Solutré
FUISSÉ
Loché
Leynes
Vinzelles
Chaintré
ST. AMOUR
JULIÉNAS
Pontanevaux
La Chapelle
CHÉNAS
FLEURIE
MOULIN À VENT
Romanèche-Thorins
CHIROUBLES
Lancié
Villié-Morgon
Beaujeu
CÔTE DE BROUILLY
MORGON
St-Lager
BROUILLY
Belleville
Odenas
Vaux
St. Georges-de-Reneins
St. Julien
Montmelas
Chambost-Allières
Villefranche
Jarnioux
Lierques
Anse
Lachassagne
Les Olmes
Chessy
Chazay
Bully

N

Saône
N 6
A 6

BROUILLY the nine 'crus' of Beaujolais

vineyards
wine route
10 km

Paris

is inferior in quality and finesse to the white.

There is one especially good white Mâcon, Pouilly-Fuissé, taking its name from the two wine villages of Pouilly and Fuissé, but also grown at the foot of the cliffs at Solutré. It is a greenish-gold wine, caressing on the tongue, but with more depth and mettle to it than might be thought at first acquaintance; a really great white Burgundy. The less impressive white Mâcons are sold simply as *Mâcon blanc*, and also as *Bourgogne blanc*, without further qualification. If they have 11% alcohol then they can be labelled as Mâcon Supérieur or Mâcon-Villages. All white Mâcons are made from the Chardonnay grape. This might be termed the proto-grape of the Mâconnais, for it came originally from the minuscule village of Chardonnay, hidden among the vineyards.

The vineyards of Mâcon shade imperceptibly into those of Beaujolais. The latter district is the most recent wine-growing area of France. It was not until the eighteenth century that the woods that once clothed the hills now draped with vineyards were cut down.

It is a vast wine district producing round about 600,000 hectolitres a year, that is to say 75 million bottles – which should reassure those who fear that the yield might be insufficient to fill all the bottles labelled as Beaujolais. Half of all this Beaujolais production consists of humbler sorts entitled only to the name of Beaujolais plain and unadorned. This is light, pleasantly fruity wine drunk young and chilled; it can be sold as Beaujolais *nouveau* only six weeks after the vintage. It is a wine wholly without pretentions, the carafe wine of the Parisian terraces, a jovial, hail-fellow-well-met of a wine that

goes with chicken and cheese, with beefsteak and brisket, with pâté and fondue, and tastes well morning, noon and night. If conditions are so favourable – as often happens in good years – that these simple Beaujolais have an alcoholic strength above 10% then they may be sold as Beaujolais Supérieur.

Beaujolais Primeur is a wine of particular charm. It is an ordinary Beaujolais in which the skins are allowed to ferment with the must for only a very brief period. This produces a fresh, uncomplicated wine that is drinkable about six weeks after vintage. However, it does not keep. Beaujolais Primeur is also interesting for the winelover since it gives an indication of the quality of the new vintage. In the centre of the Beaujolais district there are twenty-seven villages situated on granite

where soil conditions are so favourable that the wines grown here are of consistently better quality than the run of Beaujolais. To improve their quality still further these vines are rather more drastically pruned than is usual. Wine from these twenty-seven villages is entitled to be called Beaujolais-Villages, sometimes coupled with the name of the individual village of origin. These are often wines that epitomize all the charms of Beaujolais: light, translucent red in colour, they have the scent of ripe fruit and a juicy taste in which the grape is still discernible, an honest, perhaps somewhat rustic character, and they are of a disarming freshness.

Finally there are the famous nine *crus* of Beaujolais, the gentry as it were, bearing the name of their village or *côte,* not just an unqualified 'Beaujolais'. They include some particularly beautiful wines that are a delight for eye, nose and palate. They have the youthful charm characteristic of all Beaujolais (these growths can age, but they are usually drunk young, at three to four years at the most), but behind this lies the distinction and appeal of a wine of quality. Each *cru* has its own individual character attributable to the nature of the soil it grows in, and especially the degree to which the underlying

granite has been weathered. The nine are:

Brouilly   Deep in colour for a Beaujolais and quite robust and spicy in flavour.
Côte de Brouilly   Similar to the Brouilly, but headier.
Chénas   Beautiful translucent colour, soft and fruity, ages well.
Chiroubles   Good sturdy wine, well balanced, with a fine aroma of violets.
Fleurie   Light, silky, smells of peonies.
Juliénas   Robust, deep ruby-red wine, the only Beaujolais that should not be drunk young.
Morgon   Clear light red, a 'meaty', substantial wine that fills the mouth.
Moulin-à-Vent   Firm, robust, at its best comes very close to a Burgundy, ages excellently.
St-Amour   Fruity, a good deep colour.

All the wines of Beaujolais are made from the Gamay grape. Although here and there a white Beaujolais is made from this black grape it is no more than a curiosity. A white Beaujolais always tastes as if it should have been red.

Jura

Vin jaune *in* clavelins,
Château Châlon

The wine-growing area along the western slopes of the Jura mountains is small but suffused with viticultural history, and some of the most remarkable wines of all France are made here. Henry IV of France sent Jura wine to his mistress Gabrielle d'Estrées because its effects on a woman's affections were well known. Viticulture all over the world is enormously indebted to two men from the Jura: Alexis Millardet who during the phylloxera epidemic hit on the idea of grafting European vines onto North American stock; and Louis Pasteur who fathomed the secrets of yeast cells in his small vineyard near Arbois and in his home laboratory.

The best wine of the Jura is the *vin jaune*, a deep, golden-yellow wine from the Savagnin grape, which in all probability was introduced from Hungary in the Middle Ages. Unfortunately no more than 300 hectolitres per year is produced and so it remains a rare and expensive wine. It is matured in the cask for at least five years and during this time it grows a mould that is closely akin to the *flor* on sherry (see page 114). How this mould arrived in the Jura is still a mystery – one suggestion is that the spores were brought by the Spanish soldiers who occupied the country in the sixteenth century. *Vin jaune* is an enchanting wine with a ripe, nutty flavour and an aftertaste that with its

suggestion of Jura Gruyère and new nuts remains in the mouth for a good minute. The best comes from Château-Châlon, which is a village not a château. The squat local bottles called *clavelins* are used for *vin jaune*.

A second curiosity is the *vin de paille*, made from grapes picked at the end of November, spread on straw mats and then pressed in February. This wine too is aged in the cask, preferably for at least ten years. *Vins de paille* are of a deep golden colour, are almost excessively rich in flavour and aroma, and have something of the spicy character of a Tokay – perhaps due to the Hungarian origin of the Savagnin grape.

Finally there are the rosé wines of the Jura, well flavoured and with a hint of earthiness (Rosé d'Arbois is the best) and iridescent whites with a natural tendency to become sparkling, the result of the chalk soil.

Paris ●

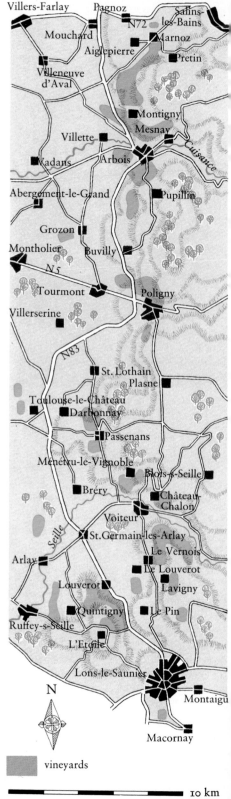

vineyards

10 km

Southeast France and Corsica

LANGUEDOC

Between the Rhône, the Mediterranean and the Pyrenees is the ancient country of Oc where a language much older than French is spoken. This is the country of the Languedoc, so called because the affirmative, in a language that combines the sonorousness of Spanish with the musical qualities of French, is *oc* instead of *oui*. This was the country where French culture began, a region of poets and troubadours. And also of the Albigensians, rebellious nobles, a branch of the Cathari, who rejected the authority of the Pope and the king of France alike. They ensconced themselves in their castles, practised their religion in their own, non-sacramental way (in a number of countries names derived from 'Cathar' were applied by the Catholic Church to all heretics), and were eventually rooted out by

military force and the Inquisition. This country is the great wine store of France where for long centuries the *vins ordinaires* have been produced – except in the small coastal districts around Banyuls and Frontignan where sweet dessert wines are made. Since World War II a number of the wines, notably those from Corbières-Roussillon and Minervois, have been so improved that they are now entitled to the classification *vins délimités de qualité supérieure*. This development towards wines of better quality is continuing and doubtless other wines will earn the right to a VDQS rating. They will never be great wines, but decent ones, cheap and reliable, agreeable for everyday use.

The great majority of wines of this region are red, robust and full-bodied, sometimes with a pleasant spiciness. They suit charcoal-grilled meat, highly seasoned dishes in which the

Vintage in Provence

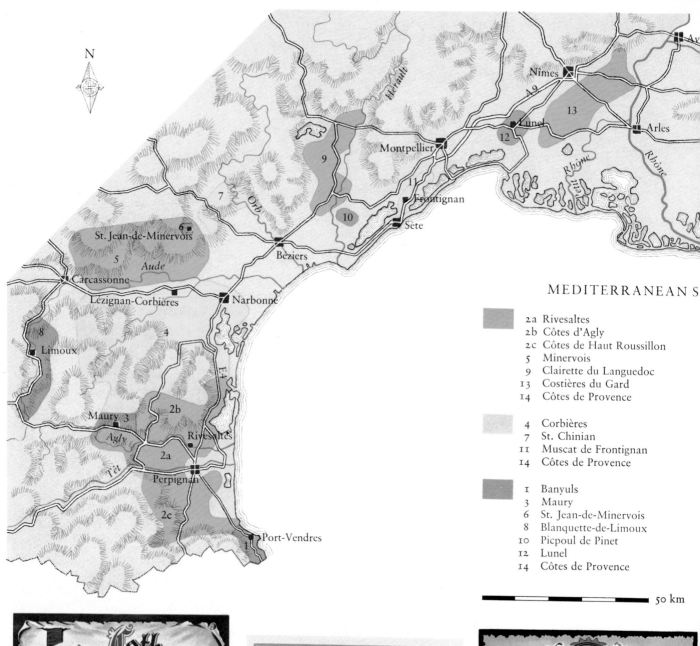

N

Ay

Nîmes

A9

Lunel 13 Arles

Montpellier 12 Rhône

Héraut Rhône

9

11 Frontignan

7 10

Orb Sète

6 St. Jean-de-Minervois

5 Aude Béziers

Carcassonne

Lézignan-Corbières Narbonne

8 4

Limoux

2b

Maury 3

Agly Rivesaltes

Tèt 2a

Perpignan

2c

1 Port-Vendres

MEDITERRANEAN S

	2a	Rivesaltes
	2b	Côtes d'Agly
	2c	Côtes de Haut Roussillon
	5	Minervois
	9	Clairette du Languedoc
	13	Costières du Gard
	14	Côtes de Provence

	4	Corbières
	7	St. Chinian
	11	Muscat de Frontignan
	14	Côtes de Provence

	1	Banyuls
	3	Maury
	6	St. Jean-de-Minervois
	8	Blanquette-de-Limoux
	10	Picpoul de Pinet
	12	Lunel
	14	Côtes de Provence

50 km

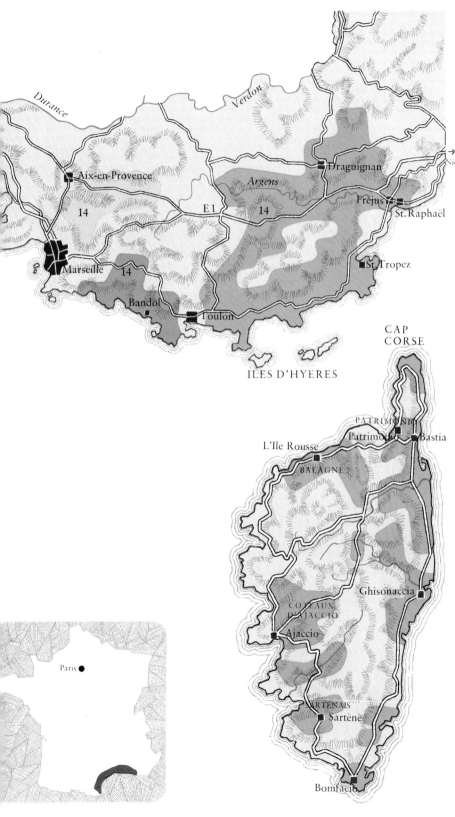

garlic has not been spared, and strong-flavoured cheeses. They are wines that will hold their own with the most penetrating aromas. The area also grows pleasant, spicy rosés and whites that conjure up a memory of stones in the hot sun.

CÔTES DE PROVENCE

Further east, between the edge of the Alps and the Rhône, lie the vineyards of the Côtes de Provence. In warm summer nights the cicadas sing in their thousands and in autumn the hillsides smell of herbs – basil, thyme, rosemary, bay and oregano. Here are grown wines entitled to the VDQS classification and often sold in decorative bottles modelled on the Greek amphoras. Spicy-scented reds, genial rosés, drier than such wines usually are, and delightful whites that partner the famous *bouillabaisse*, the fish soup of Marseille.

CORSICA

Out in the blue Mediterranean is Corsica, which would never have earned its sobriquet 'Isle of Beauty' if wine did not grow there. Corsica is an ancient wineland: cheap wine for the plebeian taverns of old Rome was fetched from here. Today many Corsican wines have attained VDQS status. There are some very fair whites which approach the Ligurian wines of Italy in type, and also good reds, such as the Royal Corse from the Bastia district. Corsican rosé is a favourite of the many tourists who come to the island in search of the sun.

vineyards

50 km

Germany

Germany comes eleventh among wine-growing countries for quantity of wine produced, but it would rank much higher in any order of quality.

The great majority of German wines are white, because of climatic and soil conditions. Here and there, however, there is some red, as in Baden-Württemberg and, remarkably, in the most northerly wine district of Germany and of all Europe – the Ahr valley where a singular light-red wine is grown on old volcanic soil; it has the somewhat bitter aftertaste of all wines of such origin.

German and French wines differ in one important principle. French wines stand or fall by their alcoholic strength, so much so that there is a prescribed minimum for each *Appellation Contrôlée*. Alcoholic strength is much less important for German wines – it is practically never stated on labels – because the vital factor is acidity. If the acidity is right a German wine can attain a great age. In the Ratskeller in Bremen, the biggest vinothèque in the country, where all German wines of any significance are to be found, and tasted, there are splendid examples from 1920, the most fabulous year for German wines this century; and the writer has even drunk a 1727 Rüdesheimer there which proved to be a very vigorous old aristocrat.

The vine conquered the sunny hillsides of the Rhine and the Moselle in the wake of the Roman legions and became established in the Palatinate (Rheinpfalz), where spring comes one month earlier than in the rest of Germany. In the fourth century AD craft of the type represented by the famous Neumagen wine ship transported casks of wine over the Moselle.

During the chaotic age of the barbarian migrations the vineyards were trampled and burned by Germanic peoples on the move, but they sprang up again in all their glory when the Emperor Charlemagne had taken matters into his firm hands. And despite all the brutish uncertainties of those early Middle Ages he managed not to overlook the cultivation of the vine; Charlemagne was, after all, very fond of cheese and consequently a lover of wine.

Nearly all the most familiar German wines come from the big wine-growing districts: the Moselle, Rheingau, Rheinhessen, the Palatinate and Franconia. But there are other German winelands, for example the Middle Rhine (Mittelrhein), between Bonn and Koblenz, where the ruins of old robber-baron castles stand romantically among the vines, and where the golden-haired Loreley once lured boatmen to their doom with her singing. The slopes are so steep and difficult to work (significantly the word for vineyard here is *Weinberg*, 'wine hill') that if anyone wants to wish his neighbour ill he says 'I hope you inherit a vineyard!' Then there is Baden-Württemberg, where the vines grow on the hills of the Black Forest, along the Neckar river and on the Kaiserstuhl, the old volcano overlooking the Rhine, and beside Lake Constance, the Bodensee of the Germans.

The Neumagen wine ship

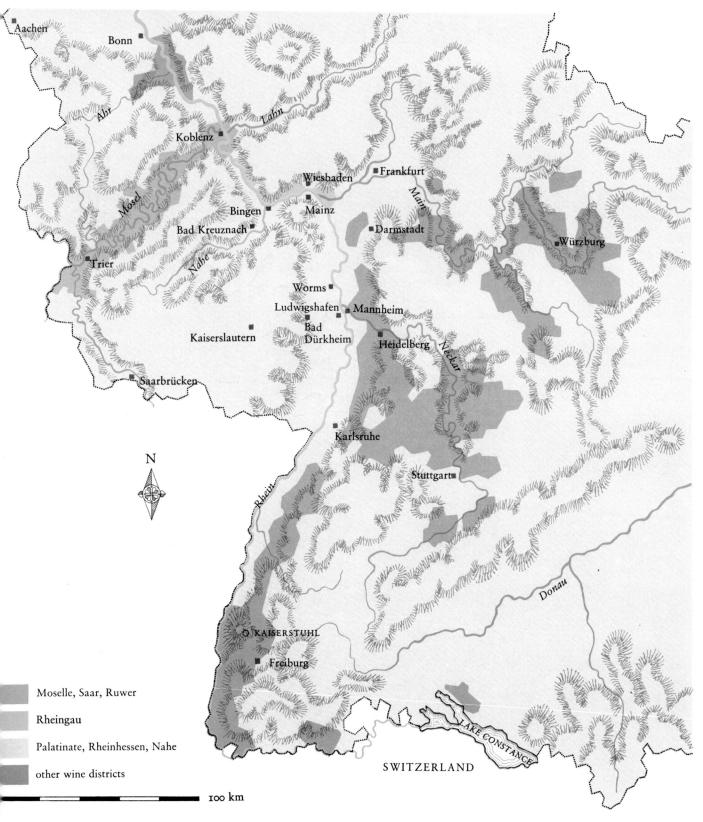

Aachen
Bonn
Ahr
Koblenz
Lahn
Mosel
Wiesbaden
Frankfurt
Bingen
Mainz
Main
Bad Kreuznach
Darmstadt
Würzburg
Nahe
Trier
Worms
Ludwigshafen
Mannheim
Kaiserslautern
Bad
Dürkheim
Heidelberg
Neckar
N
Saarbrücken
Karlsruhe
Stuttgart
Rhein
Donau
O KAISERSTUHL
Freiburg
LAKE CONSTANCE
SWITZERLAND

Moselle, Saar, Ruwer

Rheingau

Palatinate, Rheinhessen, Nahe

other wine districts

100 km

Moselle (with Luxembourg), Saar and Ruwer

Mosella, the little Meuse, was the name given by Roman legionaries to the river that rises in the Vosges and after a long series of bends and curves pours itself into the cool waters of the Rhine. The inviting green hills called out for wine growing and there appear to have been vineyards along the Moselle by the third century AD. Ausonius from Bordeaux, whose task here was to instruct the sons of Roman emperors and generals in the noble art of oratory, grew lyrical about the vineyards around Trier: 'I believe that here on the banks of this stream the shaggy satyrs must have met the blue-eyed nymphs.' In those late Roman days the Moselle provided wine for the legions stationed along this northern frontier of the empire, for not many vines grew along the Rhine at that date. In the course of the centuries the Mosella of the Romans became the Mosel of the Germans and the Moselle of the French. Its winding course has been tamed and brought under control, but the vines still climb its steep, slaty hillsides.

The Moselle becomes a wine river at the point where it begins to form the border between Luxembourg and Germany. Today there are commendable Luxembourg Moselles as well as German ones. The reputation of Luxembourg wines really dates from shortly after World War II. For many centuries the small wines from the attractive little communities of Grevenmacher, Remerschen, Wormeldange and Remich were either drunk locally or contributed anonymously to cheap German Moselles or Sekt. After the war, however, the whole Luxembourg wine industry was reorganized under the inspiring leadership of an energetic government minister. A state viticultural research station was set up, legislation was passed to regularize and protect the use of Luxembourg wine names, and high-quality vines were planted. In short the people of this tiny country succeeded in a few years in greatly developing the potential of their hitherto little-known wines. Today the Riesling, Traminer, Auxerrois (a Pinot Blanc), and in particular the Riesling x Sylvaner that does so well in Luxembourg, all flourish along the Moselle. Superior

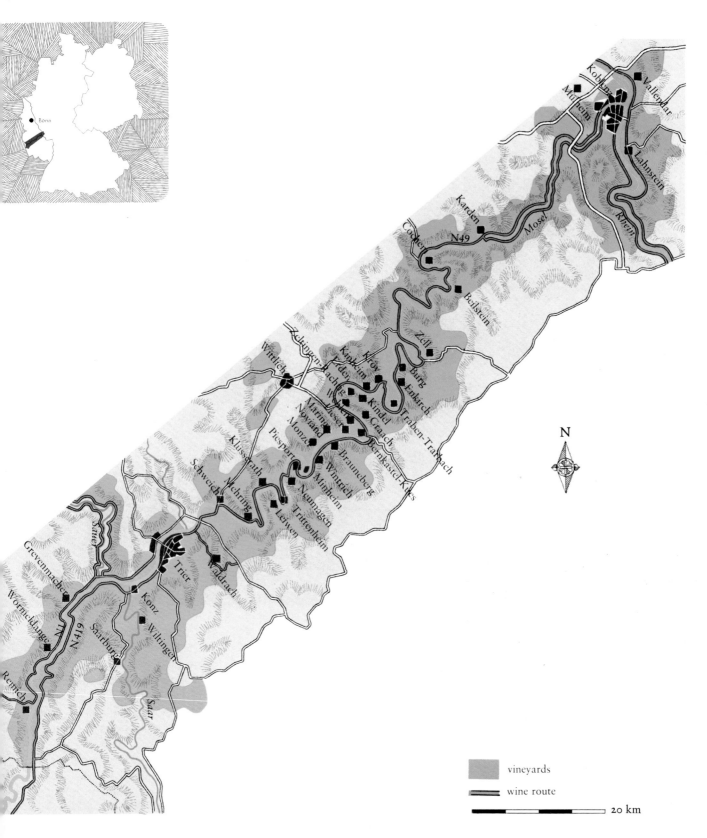

Bonn

Koblenz
Vallendar
Mülheim
Lahnstein
Rhein
Karden
N49
Mosel
Cochem
Beilstein
Zell
Burg
Wittlich
Zeltingen-Rachtig
Enkirch
Kinheim
Kröv
Ürzig
Kindel
Traben-Trarbach
Marinus
Lieser
Graach
Növiand
Bernkastel-Kues
Kluss'rath
Monzel
Braunberg
Piesport
Wintrich
Schweich
Mehring
Minheim
Neumagen
Trittenheim
Trier
Leiwen
Waldrach
Sauer
Grevenmacher
Konz
Wiltingen
Wormeldange
N419
Saarburg
Saar
Remich

N

vineyards

wine route

20 km

99

Type of hut used by vineyard workers

wines carry a seal, the *Marque Nationale*, which guarantees their origin and quality. All the wines are named after their grape variety. The ordinary, everyday Luxembourg wine is the Elbling, light, unpretentious, something to quench summer-holiday thirsts; the best is the Riesling. Luxembourg Moselles are very light (usually with an alcoholic strength of about 10%), fragrant, fresh and delicate, and good value for their moderate prices.

The wines of Luxembourg have a natural tendency to secondary fermentation and decent sparkling wines are made by the *méthode champenoise*. There is also a slightly sparkling wine, the *perlé*, but this is of lesser quality as a rule.

At Trier the Moselle enters German territory. It remains a wine river down to Koblenz. Its steep hillsides are dark in winter and early spring,

100

green in late spring and summer, and then gold in autumn. The small towns and villages have half-timbered houses, red geraniums, and everywhere there are *Weinstuben*, wine taverns where at wooden tables you can drink Moselle wine from the big, half-pint *Schoppen* and order the so-called wine grower's lunch, a wooden platter of dark wholemeal bread and excellent sausage. All the ordinary Moselles taste delightfully fresh, light and fragrant, particularly with any kind of pork meat.

The best Moselles grow in the Middle Moselle, where some thirty-seven miles of winding river is contained within the valley between Klüsserath and Enkirch, a crow's flight distance of not more than eighteen miles. This is where the famous villages are: Trittenheim, Neumagen, Dhron, Piesport, Wintrich, Brauneberg, Bernkastel, Uerzig, Kröv and Traben-Trarbach; to which every Moselle lover responds with the name of the most renowned vineyard of each – respectively Altärchen, Laudamusberg, Häschen, Treppchen, Herrgottswein, Juffer, Doktor, Würzgarten, Nacktarsch and Schlossberg. Not that all the wines that bear these illustrious names on their labels actually come from the vineyard in question. Many site names have become a sort of brandname by association for wines from a particular

village, as has been the case with Zeller Schwarze Katz. This once indicated a vineyard; now it is a generic name for wines from the village of Zell, which lies just outside the Middle Moselle area.

In 1787 the Elector Clemenz Wenzeslaus of Trier decreed that henceforth only Riesling vines should be planted in the Moselle. This was a wise decision for grown on the weathered slate of the Moselle valley and in its cool, northerly climate, the Riesling can develop its full potential. A good Moselle wine is a small miracle of flower-scented tenderness and freshness. Moselles are very light wines, seldom exceeding an alcoholic strength of 10%. Their great charm is their fruitiness combined with a delicate astringency, although many *Spätlesen*, the wines made from late-picked, overripe grapes, are rather sweet – too sweet for many lovers of Moselle. But there are some truly beautiful wines among them. Although Moselle wines can be drunk quite young the high-quality examples of a good year will always age very well.

In the Upper and Lower Moselle other vines besides the Riesling are grown, for example the Elbling and Müller-Thurgau (the Riesling-Sylvaner cross or the Rivaner as this hybrid is known in Luxembourg), but these are not used for the best

wines. They go into Moselblümchen or other unspecified ordinary wines, or into the well-known Sekt, the German sparkling wine.

Two tributaries of the Moselle are so much part of this region that their wines are always mentioned in the same breath as the Moselles. These are the Saar and Ruwer. They are both problem areas, too often affected by poor, cold summers. But when there is a good season the wines of the Saar and Ruwer can match the best Moselles. A Ruwer of a good vintage, especially one from the neighbourhood of Kasel, is a magnificent wine with an almost incredible subtlety and finesse. Saar wines too can be outstanding in a good year that enables them to develop fully their natural, honey-scented sweetness. One of the best-known Saar wine villages is Ockfen. The wise emperor Probus, who had vineyards established all along the Roman frontiers on the Continent, was fond of visiting the Saar in the time of the vintage in order to go hunting in the forests and drink the local wines in the evenings. He must have been a man of taste.

The Palatinate, Rheinhessen, Nahe and Franconia

THE PALATINATE

Once the Palatinate was honoured by the title of 'the wine cellar of the Holy Roman Empire'. Today it is still the largest German wine district, accounting for around 15% of the country's total wine production. It is an extensive area, stretching from the Rhine westwards over the Haardt mountains. The road that winds through the vineyards and over the hills, by way of such cheerful wine villages as Deidesheim, Wachenheim and Bad Dürkheim, is known as the Weinstrasse. It is a wine district of which many have heard, but it has never become so much of a tourist area as the Moselle, the Middle Rhine or the Rheingau, although there is a good deal worth seeing there. For example the Dürkheim wine cask, the largest cask in the world with a capacity of 1·7 million litres. Its

contents, however, are not wine but wine drinkers, for it is a *Weinstube*. Then there is the wine museum in Speyer (or Spires), and the cathedral with its big sandstone basin which was filled with wine whenever a new bishop was installed and from which the citizens could help themselves.

The southern part of the Palatinate is a region of quite ordinary wines. Many different varieties of vines are grown together and the wine they yield is for home consumption and for drinking young, even before fermentation is complete and it is still sweet and unimaginably heady (but excellent with the first of the new chestnuts and other nuts). It is called Federweisser and is a rather coarse, bucolic wine, but in an atmospheric *Weinstube* it has its attractions. Further north, however, near Ruppertsberg and Deidesheim, things are different. The indiscriminate mixture of vines

gives way largely to Rieslings. This is an area of good, even very high quality wines. This is due to the geology of the Middle Haardt, an old volcanic zone with a good deal of basalt and a soil rich in potash. It also has a warm, dry climate in which almond and fig trees thrive and peaches are in blossom in early spring. Soil and climate combine to make the Riesling wines that grow here barely recognizable as such, so rich, heavy and full bodied are they. Even an ordinary Sylvaner here takes on a surprising, rounded velvety softness. The great Palatinate wines are without doubt the headiest and heaviest of Germany; and the beautiful, but unfortunately costly, *Trockenbeerenauslesen* are as thick and sweet as golden honey in the glass.

RHEINHESSEN

Rheinhessen lies on the west bank of the Rhine and extends roughly from Worms to Bingen. The chief vine here is the Sylvaner, with quite a few Rieslings in the south. The wines of Rheinhessen are perhaps the friendliest Rhineland wines. The Rhine wine that is best known throughout the world comes from this district – Liebfraumilch. Originally this was grown in one particular vineyard at the foot of a mighty

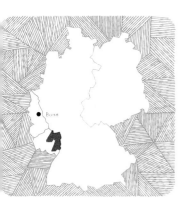

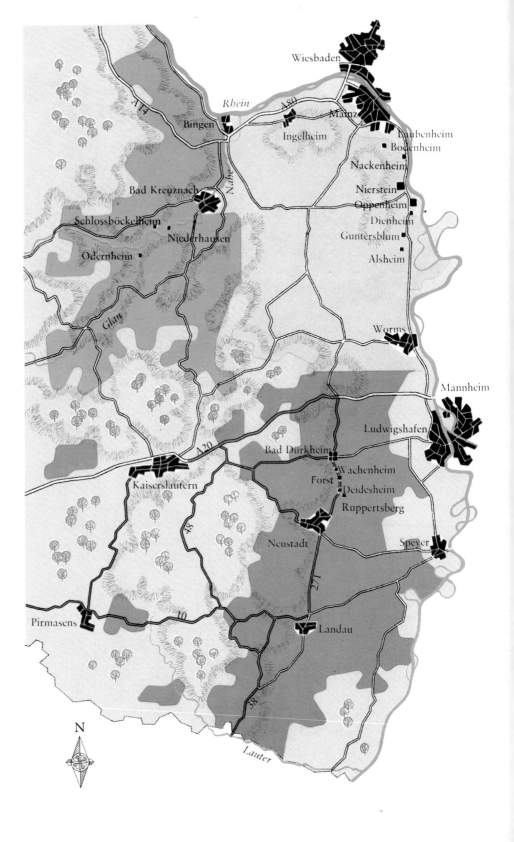

Nahe

Rheinhessen

Palatinate

wine route

25 km

Gothic church, the Liebfrauenkirche in Worms, and was a lovely, golden Rhine wine. However, 'Liebfraumilch' appealed so strongly to the imagination that the name began to take over from the wine. Soon it was the name that people wanted to drink and they did not trouble too much about which wine it was applied to. Gradually Liebfraumilch came to be a generic term for ordinary, but drinkable wines from anywhere in Rheinhessen.

From the red sandstone slopes of the Rothenberg south of Nackenheim come some particularly good wines. In Nackenheim itself there are still some of those old-fashioned wine firms that have not yet fallen victim to mechanization and streamlining, where wine is made by the traditional craft methods – increasingly uncommon in Germany. Nackenheimer Rothenberg or Rosenberg is worth looking out for. Good, agreeable Rheinhessen wines are grown in Oppenheim and Nierstein. These are full-bodied, not completely dry, pleasant of scent and mellow on the tongue. And in the appropriate way in which nature often arranges these things, thick white asparagus grows at the bottom of the vineclad slopes near Oppenheim and the wine and the vegetable make excellent partners at a meal.

NAHE

At Bingen the Rhine is joined by a tributary that has to make its way past a number of obstacles in its course. It is just where these obstacles occur that the good wines grow, notably at the foot of the enormous rust-red cliff at Bad Münster, the Rotenfels as it is called, and at Schlossböckelheim. The best-known place along this river is Bad

Kreuznach, a spa that has outlived its original purpose. Nahe wines are among the pleasantest and most interesting of German wines. Good Nahe wine is ripe and masculine, but preserves an underlying youthful freshness. Nahe wines are never heady or heavy, and in spite of their full-bodied character they have an elegance that is fairly rare in German wines.

The Liebfrauenkirche, Worms, with the famous vineyard where Liebfraumilch originated

FRANCONIA

The Franconian vineyards are situated
on the sunny hills along the river
Main, especially around the
beautiful Baroque town of Würzburg.
Remarkably enough it is the Sylvaner
not the Riesling that produces the
best wines here; this is due to the
composition of the soil, which is very
chalky. Anyone who knows the light,
fresh Sylvaners of Alsace will have
some difficulty in believing that these
Franconian wines, with their often
rather harsh dryness and their fine
but penetrating bouquet, come from
the same grape. Franconian wines
are bottled in the odd, flat
Bocksbeutel, said to have been the
invention of nuns of the Juliusspital
in Würzburg, who often used
wine from the convent vineyards
(still among the best Franconian wines)
in their ministrations to the sick.
The flat shape was easier to carry in a
large pocket in their habits. Franconian
wines are often called *Steinweine*,
after the famous vineyard of Stein by
the banks of the Main at Würzburg.
Real *Steinweine* from this vineyard
are rare. Genuine ones are
practically immortal: they could,
it has been alleged, last for four
hundred years. The only wine ever to
have achieved this age is a Tokay –
grown in totally different soil and
made from totally different grapes.

The Rhine at Kaub

Rheingau

The Rhine, after turning sharply below Mainz to flow westwards for some miles as a very broad river, is checked at Bingen by the outliers of the Hunsrück and forced to change direction north in a welter of turbulent water. This is where the Rheingau lies, Germany's most beautiful wine district, sheltered against north winds by the Taunus mountains and bathed by the sun that sparkles on the broad mirror of the Rhine. Here are the world-renowned villages of Rüdesheim, Geisenheim (where the national viticultural college is situated), Johannisberg, Oestrich, Hattenheim, Erbach and Eltville. The vine here is the Riesling, brought to the Rheingau in the twelfth century by Hildegard, abbess of the convent near Rüdesheim that bears her name – Sankt Hildegardis. The district boasts such imposing estates as Count von Matuschka-Greiffenclau's

Schloss Vollrads; Schloss Johannisberg, the property of the Metternich family; and Schloss Reinhartshausen, now a luxury hotel, which once belonged to Princess Marianne of the Netherlands.

In front of Schloss Johannisberg stands an equestrian statue of an eighteenth-century courier who was unintentionally responsible for the wines of this estate achieving their supreme glory and fame. The castle

at that time belonged to the prince-bishop of Fulda, without whose permission the grape harvest could not begin. At the beginning of October each year a messenger set off with samples of the grapes so that the bishop could ascertain their sweetness and thereby fix the date of the harvest. In 1775, however, the monks who then inhabited the *Schloss* found that they had to wait a long time for the messenger to return with the bishop's

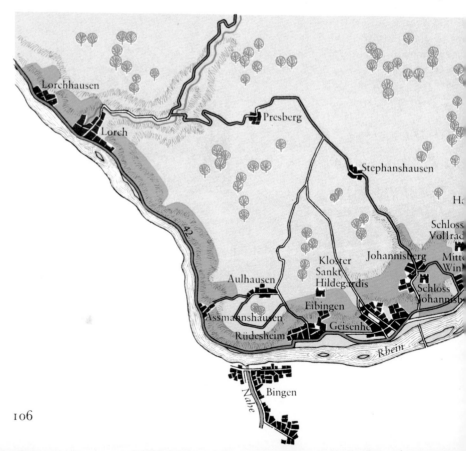

command: he had duly received the instruction but had been taken by brigands and was being held in a forest cave. In the meantime the grapes remained unpicked, they became overripe and were affected by a grey mould, and they dried up. As time went by and the courier still did not appear, the distraught monks began to pick the grapes. Full of misgiving they made wine from these shrivelled-up, unpleasant-looking articles. When at last the messenger was released by the brigands and arrived at the castle the wine had already been made. But there had never been such a wonderful golden wine, with the perfume of honey and the scent of fruit, and a rich autumnal taste of herbs and spices. It was the first *Trockenbeerenauslese* and the greyish mould was of course the *Botrytis cinerea*, the same agent that produces Sauternes. Unfortunately these *Trockenbeerenauslesen* are so rare (the *pourriture noble* appears on average only once in every four years) that they have become extremely expensive, even in Germany.

In their ripe, golden luxuriousness Rheingauers are rather old-fashioned, romantic wines. But they are great wines, wines with the aristocratic grace and allure to enhance especially festive summer evenings.

The village of Hochheim lies just outside this district, but its wines are so similar to those of the Rheingau in standard and character that they are always classed as Rheingauers. In the English-speaking world 'hock', said to be a corruption and abbreviation of Hochheimer, became the general term for white wine from the Rhineland. The Hochheim site of Königin Victoria Berg was so named when its owners learned of Queen Victoria's fondness for hock.

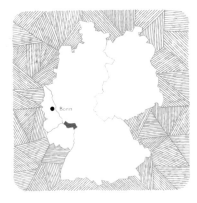

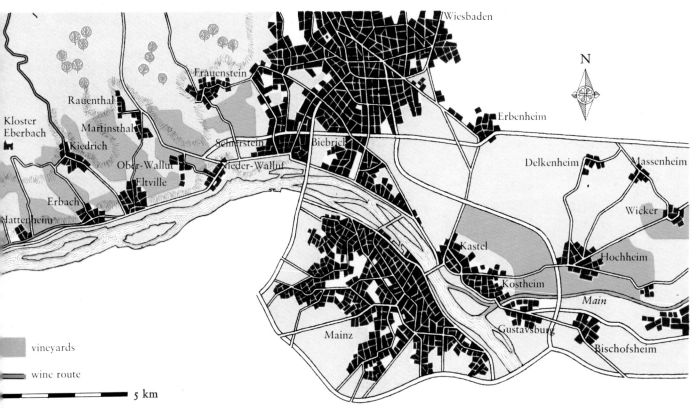

vineyards

wine route

5 km

Spain and Portugal

Spain and Portugal are very ancient wine-producing countries; Spain was the great supplier to imperial Rome. By about the second century AD the port of Ostia, where most of Rome's imports of food and drink came in, had apparently handled more than two million amphoras of Spanish wine. It came principally from Valencia and Tarragona. Today Spain is the third biggest wine producer in the world. The annual production is more than 25 million hectolitres.

There is no part of Spain without wine. In the extreme northwest, in green, cool Galicia, there is the light, white Ribeiro which goes well with anything caught in the rocky bays of the Galician coast. In Navarre there is the well-liked Rioja; in León the heavy red Toro; along the Catalonian coast the sweet wines of Tarragona, the sparkling wines of Panadés and

In the bodegas in Jerez wines are sometimes earmarked for illustrious customers

the gold-coloured, dry white wines served liberally in carafes in the small fish restaurants of the Costa Brava and Barcelona. Then there are the red, almost purplish-black, wines of La Mancha, land of Don Quixote; the bone-dry white of Valdepeñas; the fiery, heady wines of Estramadura; the noble sherry of Andalusia; the dark-brown, honey-sweet Málaga and the heavy, scented wines of Valencia and Requeña. Spain is an inexhaustible cellar full of good, moderately priced wines. The Spanish poet Narciso-Alonso Cortés wrote: 'This is the cellar, the most noble cellar where the wines are kept that chase away all sadness and whisper friendly counsel in our ears.' Could anything be better said about so rich a storehouse of wines?

Portugal too is a great and good wine country, a country of heart-warming

port, but also of light, tingling genial rosés, of robust table wines and the delightful *vinho verde*, and of heavy, sweet muscat wines. It is also the country of the romantic Madeira, for the island of that name, far out in the Atlantic, is a province of Portugal. It was discovered by a Portuguese expedition in 1420. Malvasia vines were introduced from Crete, Spanish vines from Andalusia, Portuguese from the port districts and Rieslings from Germany. These vines were planted on the steep slopes of volcanic rock and ash and trained up on trellises. A tiny wine-growing district, but one that yields great and interesting wines.

Wine porter on Madeira

108

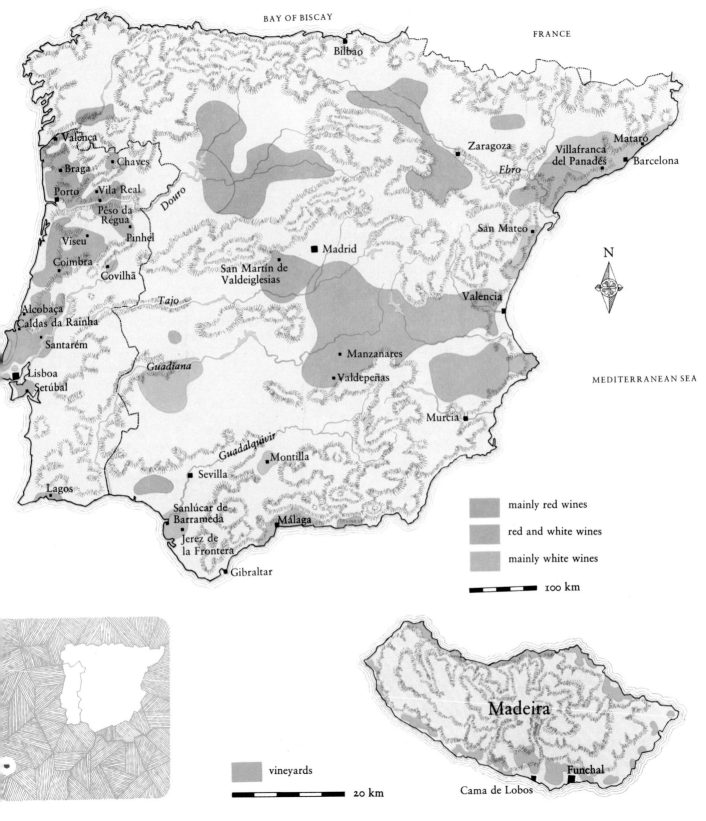

BAY OF BISCAY

FRANCE

Bilbao

Valença

Chaves

Braga

Porto

Vila Real

Peso da Régua

Douro

Pinhel

Viseu

Coimbra

Covilhã

Tajo

Alcobaça

Caldas da Rainha

Santarém

Lisboa

Setúbal

Guadiana

Lagos

Guadalquivir

Sevilla

Sanlúcar de Barrameda

Jerez de la Frontera

Gibraltar

Zaragoza

Ebro

San Mateo

Villafranca del Panadés

Mataró

Barcelona

Madrid

San Martín de Valdeiglesias

València

Manzanares

Valdepeñas

Murcia

MEDITERRANEAN SEA

Montilla

Málaga

N

mainly red wines

red and white wines

mainly white wines

100 km

vineyards

20 km

Madeira

Funchal

Cama de Lobos

Spain : Rioja

In northern Spain, along the banks of the Ebro, in the old kingdom of Navarre where Richard Lionheart found his bride, the fair Berengaria, is the wine district of Rioja. Everyone knows the name, but few the country. It is certainly not a region to attract the tourists, being a rather monotonous plateau, ringed by mountain ridges. Its name comes from that of the Rio Oja, a small tributary of the Ebro. At the centre of the region is the sleepy little town of Logroño that comes awake once a year, during the wine festival when, as part of the celebrations, the biggest eaters from a wide area around compete to see who can put away the most lamb, washed down with red Rioja. To the west of Logroño lies the Rioja Alta, or High Rioja; to the east the Rioja Baja, the Low Rioja.

The difference between the two is principally one of climate. Rioja Alta is quite damp and cool and therefore the lightest and best Riojas grow there. Rioja Baja is much warmer and drier and its wines are heavier and rather graceless. They are mostly sold not as Riojas but as ordinary, non-vintage wines. Good Riojas from the Rioja Alta have an almost un-Spanish lightness. The Spaniards like to compare them with Bordeaux wines, and in fact they do have a slightly French character and a certain elegance. This may be due to the fact that towards the end of the nineteenth century many French wine growers who had been reduced to penury by the ravages of the phylloxera in their vineyards worked for long periods in the Rioja district and passed on French methods to the Spanish growers and cellarers.

Rioja wine is still made in the old-fashioned manner, particularly with regard to the length of time it spends in the cask, even the white. The whites acquire by this means a deep gold colour and a certain ripe taste – the result of oxidization – which is much liked in Spain. For customers abroad who may prefer their white wines to have a fruity taste and a lighter character, Rioja is sometimes bottled for export rather sooner than would normally be the case. The reds benefit from their long maturing in the cask. It gives them a ripe warmth and a beautiful colour tending towards gold brown, and they lose the harshness so typical of most Spanish red wines.

The dates often printed on Rioja labels suggest a venerable age. These should not be taken too seriously or literally: although there will be some old wine in the bottle so labelled, this does not account for all the contents. Nearly all Riojas are a blend of various vintages, and usually of wine from a number of vineyards. Vineyard names are sometimes given on labels – Pomal (red wine) or Paceta (white) are examples – but these are more in the nature of brandnames that precise denominations. However, every bottle of Rioja from the Zona Vinicola Rioja, where the best vineyards are situated, carries a seal of quality from the Consejo Regulador de la Dominación Rioja.

Madrid

Lisbon

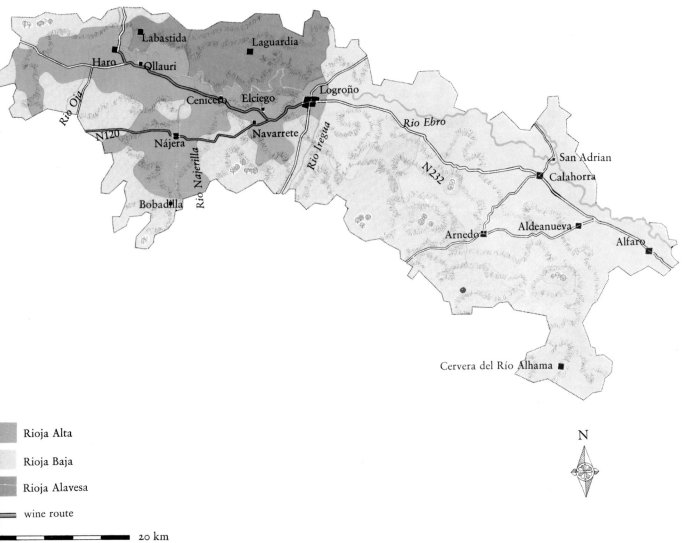

Labastida
Laguardia
Haro
Ollauri
Río Oja
Cenicero
Elciego
Logroño
N120
Navarrete
Río Ebro
Nájera
Río Najerilla
Río Iregua
San Adrian
N232
Calahorra
Bobadilla
Arnedo
Aldeanueva
Alfaro
Cervera del Río Alhama

Rioja Alta

Rioja Baja

Rioja Alavesa

wine route

20 km

N

Spain: Jerez and Montilla

Deep in Andalusia, more than sixty miles beyond Seville, there are extensive vineyards on white, dry, cracked soil under a blazing sun where the golden-green Palomino grape is grown, the grape from which sherry is made.

'Sherry' is an English corruption of the Spanish name Jerez, short for Jerez de la Frontera, the ancient, drowsy little town smelling of sherry and orange blossom where the big sherry bodegas are situated.

The English are supposed to have discovered sherry in the sixteenth century when they called at the harbours of Cadiz and Sanlúcar de Barrameda in need of salt and smelled the wine. Sherry has long been a firm British favourite. Shakespeare must have been fond of it, or so it would seem from the eulogy of sherry which he has Falstaff make in *Henry IV Part II*:

A good sherris-sack hath a twofold operation in it. It ascends me into the brain; dries me there all the foolish and dull and crudely vapours which environ it; makes it apprehensive, quick, forgetive, full of nimble, fiery, and delectable shapes; which delivered o'er to the voice, – the tongue, – which is the birth, becomes excellent wit. The second property of your excellent sherris is, – the warming of the blood. . . . If I had a thousand sons, the first human principle I would teach them should be, – to forswear thin potations, and to addict themselves to sack.

Surprisingly, the Dutch have overtaken the British and are now the world's biggest sherry drinkers, consuming 2·5 litres per person per year.

Sherry is a remarkable wine, perhaps the most interesting that there is. It is the most mysterious and nobody, not even the people of Jerez who work with it from generation to generation, can fully explain it; nor can they forecast how a particular example will turn out. Man has to wait and leave the last word with nature when it comes to sherry.

About the middle of September, when the grapes are ripe, the

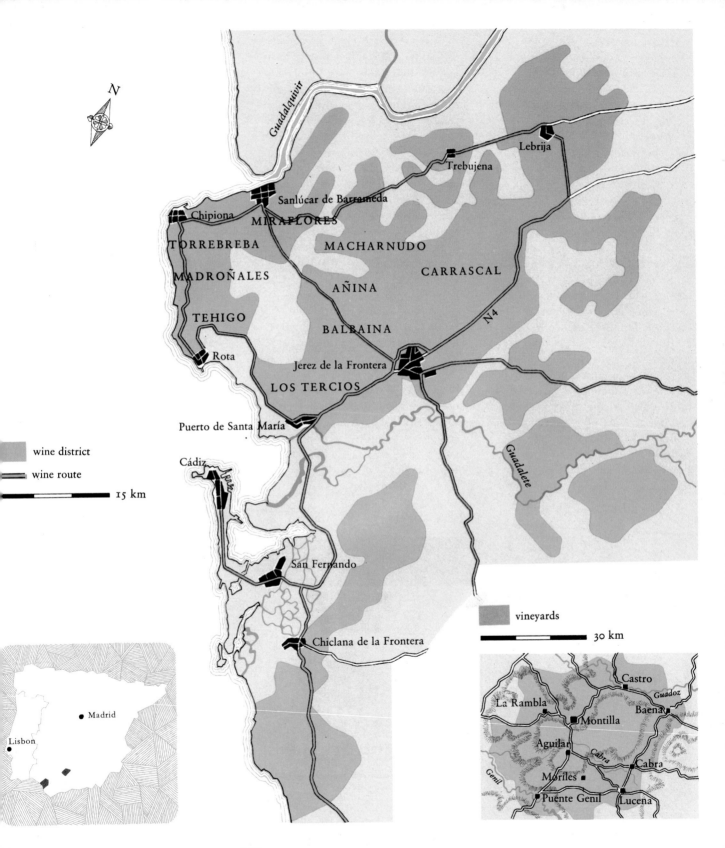

N

Guadalquivir

Lebrija

Trebujena

Sanlúcar de Barrameda

Chipiona

MIRAFLORES

MACHARNUDO

TORREBREBA

CARRASCAL

MADROÑALES

AÑINA

TEHIGO

BALBAINA

N4

Rota

Jerez de la Frontera

LOS TERCIOS

Puerto de Santa María

Cádiz

Guadalete

wine district

wine route

15 km

San Fernando

vineyards

30 km

Chiclana de la Frontera

Madrid

Castro

Guadoz

Lisbon

La Rambla

Baena

Montilla

Aguilar

Cabra

Cabra

Genil

Moriles

Puente Genil

Lucena

gitanos, the gypsies of Andalusia, come from far and near, usually in family groups, to help with the harvest. The grapes are spread out after picking on esparto-grass mats to shrivel in the sun and so increase their sweetness. In the cool of the night they are pressed – in a few places still in the traditional manner by serious, silent men in short white trousers wearing boots with soles patterned with nailheads. They tread the sweet-smelling mass of grapes and the skins and pips form a soft, springy layer between the nails of the boots. This prevents the pips being crushed and releasing tannin or other unwanted substances into the wine. However, men treading grapes on starry nights to the strumming of guitars are becoming an increasingly uncommon sight. The demand for sherry has grown so much that here too modern methods and horizontal winepresses have been introduced. Within twenty-four hours the must in the casks begins to ferment, sending thick dirty-white scum frothing through the bungholes.

When the must has become wine its long and difficult period of nurture begins. This takes place in the bodegas, vast sheds with sand floors and roofs supported by rows of whitewashed posts and arches – which is why they are often compared with cathedrals. The casks of wine are stacked up in layers according to a system known as the solera. This term is derived from a Spanish word, *solar*, difficult to translate but meaning roughly the tradition that holds a family together.

When a young wine is a few years old and has been fortified with a measure of brandy it is ready to be included in the top row of casks, the *criadera*, or nursery. After due time it can be moved to the row below, and this process is repeated until it reaches the bottom row in the system, the casks from which the sherry is drawn for sale. These casks are never completely emptied; whatever is drawn off is replenished from the next senior row of casks and so on up the solera, new wine being brought into the *criadera* at the top. In this way the shipper has a perpetual

supply of matured wine. All sherry is therefore a complex blend of wines of different vintages and from a variety of vineyards. This also explains the great range of prices possible with sherry: the more old wine and the more wine from first-class vineyards a blend contains, the more expensive it will be.

The solera is not the only peculiarity of sherry: there is also the mystery of the *flor*. While the sherry is in cask in the bodega a white mould, the *flor*, appears on it – but not in every instance, and why it does not affect all casks has not yet been satisfactorily explained. After completing its work the *flor*, a kind of white yeast, disappears. This *flor* turns the wine into sherry, giving it its characteristic colour and slightly nutty, gently bitter taste. This remarkable and essential relationship between wine and *flor* is peculiar to Andalusia – except for an isolated and so far unexplained manifestation in the Jura in France. Sherry is, as it were, a very self-willed wine and so the end result of the processes described above

is not a homogeneous commodity
but a number of types (something
quite different from brands: in sherry
these embrace more than one type)
each with a distinct character.

Fino   Sherry matured in the bodegas
of Jerez de la Frontera, generally dry,
with a fine nutty taste, light coloured;
the Spaniard's own sherry.
Amontillado   Older than a *fino*, golden
coloured, dry but so full of taste that
the dryness is hardly noticeable; the
most elegant of the sherries.
Manzanilla   Sherry matured in the
bodegas of Sanlúcar de Barrameda,
very light, dry, with the fine, bitter
scent of camomile flowers.
Oloroso   A sherry affected little or not
at all by the *flor*, golden brown,
rich in scent and full bodied in taste.
Although an *Oloroso* is basically dry,
a little sweet wine from another grape
variety, the Pedro Ximenes, is often
added to sweeten its taste.
Cream sherry   Very sweet, golden-
brown sherry, consisting of an
Oloroso to which a good amount of
Pedro Ximenes has been added.
There is also Pale Cream sherry,
lighter of colour and not so sweet.
Pale dry   A blend of fairly young
sherries of undistinguished origins.
Light in colour; described as dry, but
generally not completely so.

MONTILLA

In the hills east of Seville, and a long
way outside the sherry-growing area,
there lies the small wine district of
Montilla where, by another of those
inexplicable whims of nature, a wine is
grown with a strong resemblance to
sherry; golden, dry, with the fine bitter
aroma that characterizes a good
sherry. It is the wine served as an
apéritif in the small fish restaurants of
Málaga before dishes with prawns or

small octopus. Although this wine is
sometimes difficult to distinguish from
sherry, the very stringent *Consejo
Regulador* protecting the latter prohibits
it from being marketed as anything
but Montilla or Moriles. By way of
compensation, however, the noblest
of the sherries, Amontillado, derives
its name from Montilla because of the
close resemblance between them.

Virtuoso performance by a venenciador,
the man who serves sherry in a bodega

Portugal

All wines convey the flavour and atmosphere of their native soil. The Portuguese countryside is mostly green and welcoming; the Portuguese language sounds soft and friendly; and the country's wines share these qualities, and generally lack the harsh, fiery properties basic to Spanish wines.

The slightly sparkling Portuguese rosés, marketed in decorative bottles, have become very familiar. However,

these are made specially for export and are intended to suit a range of perhaps none-too-discriminating palates and they have little individual character. There are much more interesting wines in Portugal than these. There is, for example, *vinho verde*, the 'green wine' from Minho, the northernmost province. The 'green' in the name does not refer to the colour of the wine, for there is both red and white *vinho verde*, but to the grapes which grow on vines trained up on pergolas among the trees and, being thus sheltered from both direct and radiated heat, do not ripen fully. The wines from these grapes are therefore light, of a northern freshness and an agreeable acidity. As they are bottled young some secondary fermentation takes place in the bottle and they become slightly sparkling. The whites in particular are delightful wines.

The best Portuguese table wine comes from Dão (it sounds like 'dow' pronounced through the nose), a beautiful countryside south of the river Douro, where the vineyards are set among pinewoods, scented in the hot sun. Red Dão is particularly good, especially if drunk not too young – fragrant, warm, and of an honest, straightforward nature. In the sand dunes between Sintra and the Atlantic there grows another excellent wine, Colares. It has the lightness and

warmth of all wines grown on sand. This is one of the few regions that remained free of the phylloxera. A red Colares can attain a great age.

The greatest, most famous and by far the most interesting wine of Portugal, however, is port. It grows in the bleak, inaccessible and scorching valleys of the upper Douro and a number of its tributaries. Black grapes for red port grow on steep, terraced hillsides of slaty rock; white grapes for

white port grow on granite. When the grapes are beginning to ripen at the end of September musicians with pipes and drums go out through the impoverished, lonely hinterland of Tras os Montes to recruit workers for the vintage. They descend the mountain paths in long files, the musicians in the lead, the men, women and children following behind, carrying bundles of possessions and cooking pots. The women and girls go into the vineyards as pickers. The strongest men throw a jute sack over their heads with a little support made of cork on which to rest baskets filled with eighty pounds and more of grapes. The remainder, the older men and the boys, go to the *lagares*, the pressing sheds, where in the late evenings teams of twenty, thirty or even forty, their trousers rolled up, move round in the purple mass, treading the grapes for hours on end. There is justification for this time-hallowed method: bare feet leave the pips and stalks uncrushed (they would be harmful crushed) and at the same time ensure that all the colour is pressed out of the grapeskins. But even in this region the traditional methods are being replaced and machinery has been introduced.

When the dark must begins to ferment there comes the critical moment when the brandy is added. This stops fermentation so that the sugar not used up remains in the wine, which attains an alcoholic strength of 18 to 20%. After this the young wine goes into casks in cellars open to the cold winter air and the desired integration of wine and alcohol takes place. In the early days of spring the wine travels down the banks of the Douro by train or lorry – formerly it went on the picturesque river craft called *barcos rabelos* – to the lodges of the big port-shipping firms in Vilanova de Gaia, at the

mouth of the river opposite the harbour of Oporto. Most of the big shippers have been British – although there are also some eminent Portuguese houses – since the eighteenth century, when the first of them set up here. There had long been a barter trade between England and the upper Douro. The English brought dried fish, the stockfish or 'trusty friend' as the local people termed this so vital food item; the Portuguese offered wine and the exchange was made in Oporto. The port has first to mature for two years, in the Vilanova lodges, then the blender, the key figure in every port-shipping firm, makes up the various types of port from the different wines in the cellars – sometimes there are hundreds of varieties. All ports consist of a blend of wines from various grapes (these are old, indigenous types), different vineyards and

generally from different years. These are the types of port:

Ruby Red port bottled young, thus retaining its deep ruby colour. It tastes of the ripe grapes; it is warm and fruity, potent and fiery.
Tawny Red port matured in the cask. The effect of the wood and of the air that comes in through its pores is to change the ruby red colour to the golden reddish-brown suggested by the name. It acquires a rich, complex taste and a velvety quality.
Vintage port Red port, but made from wines of one particular year, stated on the bottle label. It can only be made in certain very good years; a vintage is 'declared' by individual shippers when conditions are expecially favourable. Such wines are not blended with wines of other years. Vintage port is bottled young, but needs many years, often more than

Grape harvest by oxcart in the Douro

twenty, to develop its full, mature excellence. A merchant may sell port already matured, offering to decant it, because of the deposit or 'crust' it will have thrown, into a clean bottle at the request of his customer; but often vintage port is bought young for laying down. A fully matured vintage port is the noblest product of the Douro vineyards, one of the truly great wines of the world.

White port   Although André Simon once wrote that the first duty of a port is to be red, there are white ports that some people find good. White port is softer and sweeter than red. There are no vintage whites. To meet the contemporary taste for less sweet drinks there is now a dry white port, for which the must is allowed to complete fermentation before the brandy is added.

Port of course partners nuts; but this great after-dinner drink will also go well with some cheeses and is one of the few wines that will stand being drunk with fruit: pineapple, peaches, strawberries and apricots. Finally there is Dr Johnson's famous dictum: 'Claret is the liquor for boys; port for men.'

Madeira is a remarkable and intriguing wine. Treatment that would be the death of all other wines is just right for it. The Portuguese island of Madeira was once a victualling station that served ships sailing round the Cape of Good Hope to the Indies. Wine was taken aboard and it was discovered that the ordinary, rather rough red wine of Madeira that crossed the equator in ship's holds acquired a deep golden-brown colour and a wonderfully smooth, warm taste. The practice developed of imitating the sea voyage through the tropics by ageing the wine in casks left out in the sun, later by slowly heating it for six weeks up to a temperature of 50°C, then letting it cool over the same length of time. Madeira treated in this way was found to be just as good as the wine that had crossed the equator. There are four types of Madeira:

Sercial   Made from Riesling vines imported in the eighteenth century. A light, dry, very fine and fragrant Madeira.

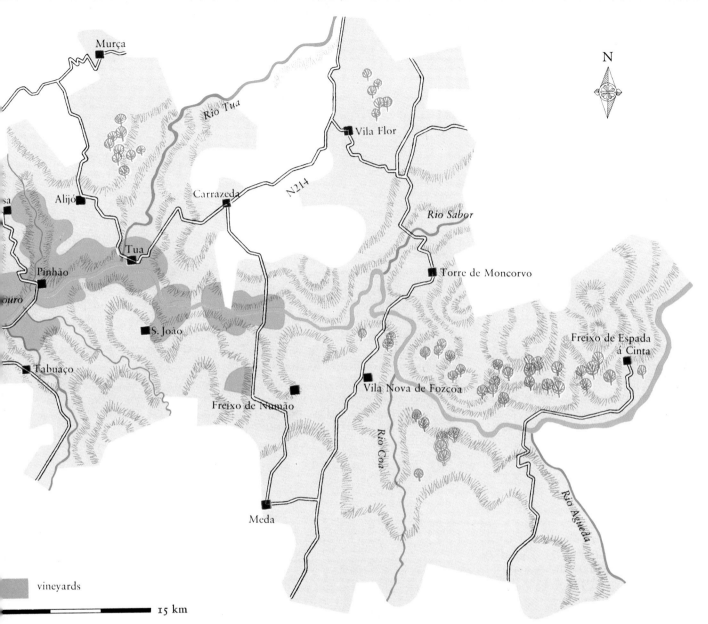

N

Rio Tua

Murça

Rio Tua

Vila Flor

N214

Alijó

Carrazeda

Rio Sabor

Tua

Torre de Moncorvo

Pinhão

Douro

Freixo de Espada
á Cinta

S. João

Vila Nova de Fozcoa

Tabuaço

Rio Côa

Freixo de Numão

Rio Agueda

Meda

vineyards

15 km

Verdelho   A soft, light and semi-sweet Madeira, sometimes a little smoky in its aftertaste. The Rainwater Madeira familiar in the United States is a blend of Sercial and Verdelho.
Boal (Bual)   The most commonly encountered Madeira, golden brown, fairly sweet but with a light, fresh aftertaste.
Malmsey   Made from the Malvasia grape, a dark-brown, heavy and very sweet Madeira.

Madeira is always blended from wines from different vineyards and different years. The blend may include some very old wine in a good quality Madeira. Examples of Madeira more than a century old can still be bought, for Madeira can achieve a venerable age.

Madrid

Lisbon

Italy

Italy could justly be called a boot full of wine. The Greeks knew it as Oenotria, 'Land of Wine', and today the country has the biggest wine production in the world: 74 million hectolitres a year. The vine grows everywhere, from the cool slopes below the snowy Alpine peaks to the hot plains of Sicily: on graceful pergolas in Tyrol and beside the North Italian lakes, spreading along wires from tree to tree in the Po valley and the Emilia, clinging to elms and pear trees in Tuscany and Umbria, in neat straight rows in Lazio and the Alban hills, in fields red with poppies in Sardinia, climbing up the dark lava flanks of Vesuvius and Etna, and in the torrid expanses of western Sicily.

The mysterious Etruscans were the people who apparently introduced the vine into Italy, before 1000 BC. Today vineyards still produce excellent wines at the feet of the volcanic hills where they first planted their vines. Chianti and Orvieto could be said to have been started on their way by the Etruscans.

In Italy wine has always been grown, made and drunk with a splendid lightheartedness. It has always been there, it is everywhere available, so why be too serious about it? This is why some Italian wines have not been as good as they could have been, and why labelling has not always been reliable. However, this carefree approach is becoming a thing of the past. Some years ago Italy began seriously to tackle the regulation of her viticulture, instituting control of the varieties of grapes planted, the number of vines per acre, of methods of cultivation and of winemaking. A start has been made in bringing some order into the confusion of Italian nomenclature. The Italian wine law of 1963 gave three types of guarantee:

Denominazione semplice, a simple designation of place of origin implying no criteria of quality; *Denominazione di origine controllata*, a seal of quality the grower himself can apply for – a committee decides whether the submitted wine merits it; and finally there is the *Denominazione controllata e garantita* for quality wines from one specified estate (what would be termed a château in, for example, Bordeaux). It will be some years

before all the country's wines of quality have been brought within this system, but the work continues steadily.

Choosing from the wines offered by Italian producers has always been a pleasurable task. Italy has some particularly attractive wines whose qualities are of course most enhanced when they are served with dishes from the rich and varied resources of the Italian cuisine.

n the Alban hills south of Rome people can
ke their food with them when they go to
y the wine at a grower's

Northern Italy

From west to east across northern Italy, like a sunny south-facing balcony, stretches the long line of the Alps. A poetic country of picture-postcard lakes, holiday villages and of vineyards, hundreds of vineyards where some of the best wines of Italy grow.

In the west is Piedmont, where the best vineyards lie in the hills between Turin and the Apennines. The Piedmontese are justly proud of their wine, especially of the two great reds, Barolo and Barbaresco. The latter wine is said to owe its name to the fact that in the centuries before Julius Caesar had conquered Gaul for Rome, tribes of Gallic barbarians were perpetually descending on Piedmont simply, it is alleged, to drink their fill of Piedmontese wine. Barolo and Barbaresco are both full-bodied, fragrant red wines, favourites in Piedmont for drinking with autumn game. Both are made from the Nebbiolo grape, so called because it is not picked until the autumn mists are in the vineyards. Two remarkable wines grown in Piedmont are Asti Spumante and vermouth. Asti Spumante is a sparkling wine from the district around Asti, made from muscat grapes. It is usually rather sweet, but the muscat aroma makes it a most agreeable wine if drunk well cooled. Turin is the chief city and centre for vermouth. Vermouth is essentially a fortified wine flavoured with herbs. Wine flavoured with herbs and spices has an ancient lineage: Hippocrates, the father of medicine, gave it to his patients 2,500 years ago and the hippocras sold by apothecaries in the Middle Ages was the same kind of preparation. Farmers' wives in Piedmont were long familiar with herb-flavoured wine as a home remedy and this gave a Turin doctor the idea of manufacturing it on a big scale for sale as an apéritif. The old peasant recipe was improved, refined and, of course, more manufacturers joined in when the wine proved successful. Each vermouth producer has his own carefully guarded secret recipe. The basis of all vermouths is a muscatel wine, which is in itself spicy. To this is added a quantity of sugar and an extract of various herbs and spices, such as

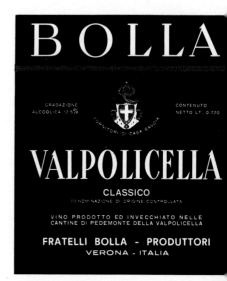

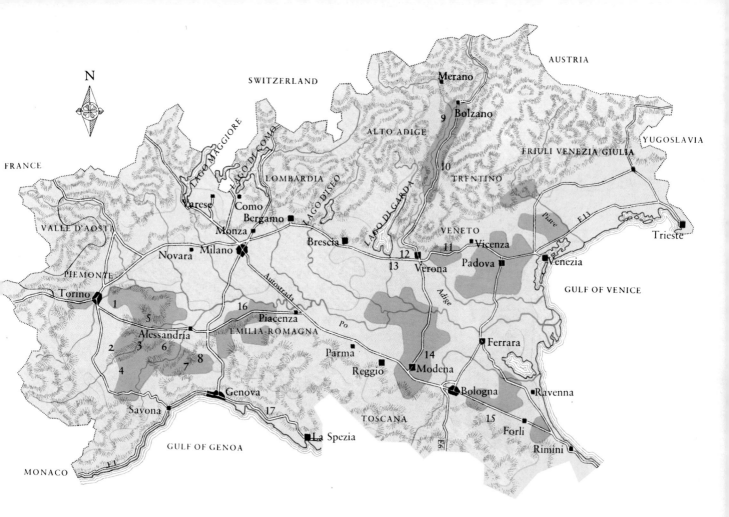

N

SWITZERLAND

AUSTRIA

FRANCE

LAGO MAGGIORE

LAGO DI COMO

LOMBARDIA

LAGO D'ISEO

MERANO

ALTO ADIGE

9 Bolzano

10

TRENTINO

FRIULI VENEZIA GIULIA

YUGOSLAVIA

VALLE D'AOSTA

Varese

Como

Bergamo

Monza

LAGO DI GARDA

VENETO

11 Vicenza

Trieste

E13

Piave

PIEMONTE

Novara

Milano

Brescia

12

13 Verona

Padova

Venezia

Torino

1

16

Adige

GULF OF VENICE

5

Piacenza

Po

14

Ferrara

Alessandria

EMILIA-ROMAGNA

Parma

Modena

2 3 6

Reggio

Bologna

Ravenna

4

7 8

Genova

Savona

17

TOSCANA

15

Forli

E3

GULF OF GENOA

La Spezia

Rimini

MONACO

E1

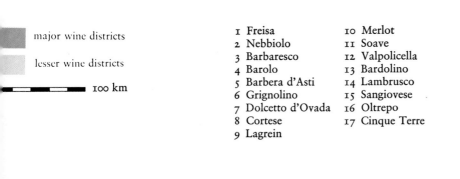

☐ major wine districts

☐ lesser wine districts

▬ 100 km

1 Freisa
2 Nebbiolo
3 Barbaresco
4 Barolo
5 Barbera d'Asti
6 Grignolino
7 Dolcetto d'Ovada
8 Cortese
9 Lagrein

10 Merlot
11 Soave
12 Valpolicella
13 Bardolino
14 Lambrusco
15 Sangiovese
16 Oltrepo
17 Cinque Terre

cinchona, coriander, gentian,
cinnamon, sage, thyme, angelica
and, most important of all, the bitter
herb wormwood. (It is the German
word for wormwood, *Wermut*, that
has given the wine its name.) There is
red vermouth, very spicy and slightly
sweet; a white, gentle and fairly sweet;
and a dry white used particularly for
cocktails.

On the shores of Lake Garda and in
the hills around Verona, the city of
star-crossed Romeo and Juliet, grow
two wines that enjoy some popularity
in other European countries, Bardolino
and Valpolicella. Bardolino, taking its
name from a pretty village on a hill
near the lake, is a light, exceedingly
pleasant red wine. It is so light red
in colour that many people mistake
it for a rosé. Bardolino is always
drunk very young; it is already
delicious a mere six weeks after the
vintage.

A good Valpolicella is a deep,
lustrous red in colour. It smells of all
the flowers in the gardens beside Lake
Garda and its greatest charm is
perhaps its gently bitter-sweet
aftertaste. There is also a Valpolicella
rosé but it has little character.
Further east, along the Soave river,
grows a wine that many people,
especially Italians, regard as the
country's best white wine. The finest
of it comes from a small area defined

as Soave classico. It is a dry white
wine, smooth and gentle, pleasantly
fresh and excellent with trout. It
should be drunk as young as possible.

If we climb upstream from the Adige
into the mountains of the Italian
Tyrol we come to Bolzano, set in an
exquisite wine district. The grapes
grow in picturesque fashion on vines
trained up on graceful pergolas and on
narrow terraces against the sides of the
mountains. The purity of cool
mountain air can be sensed in the
wines of the Alto Adige. They are
pleasant wines that are much
appreciated abroad: about half of
Italy's total wine exports come from
this region. One famous white grape,
the Traminer, originates from a wine
village among vineyards and orchards
that was called Tramin when the
area was still Austrian. One of the
best white wines of this part of Italy
is the Terlano from Merlano, but in
general this is a country of excellent
red wines, some of which, like the
Teroldego and Caldaro, are of a
beautifully deep colour. Both have a
slight aroma of almonds and cherries.
Others are a very light red, almost
rosé, such as the renowned Santa
Maddalena, with its soft hint of
bitterness in its aftertaste, and
Lagarino in which something of a
vanilla fragrance can be detected.
Vino Santo has a deep amber hue

and a spicy, honey sweetness; it is
made from grapes that are hung in
barns until Ognissanti (All Hallows,
1 November) to dry and shrivel to a
concentrated essence of sweetness.

If we descend from the mountains to
the fertile country of Emilia we see
how in this flat, green landscape the
vine tendrils reach from tree to tree
and how nicely fattened pigs root
about around thriving farms. Here too
nature has assembled things that
belong together. Emilia-Romagna is
the country where Italian cooking
reaches its peak in the towns of
Modena and Bologna. Where could
you eat such sauces with the pasta,
where such turkeys or such rice with
truffles as in Bologna; or where
could you find such inspired treatment
of everything that comes from the
pig as in Modena? If on viewing the
pink and golden-brown mountains of
sausage, ham, stuffed pig's trotters
and other delicacies in the shops and
restaurants you ask yourself anxiously
how anyone could possibly cope with
such richness and abundance, there
is an answer: with a bottle of
Lambrusco, an absolutely dry,
sparkling red wine that is equal to the
fattest pig's trotter.

Central Italy

The most famous name among Italian wines, Chianti, is the result of a mistake made by a monk in 790 when writing out a deed concerning the donation of a piece of land to the abbey of San Bartolomeo in Ripoli. The name was rendered as Clanti, but should have been Campi, that is to say 'fields'. 'Clanti' was perpetuated in later documents and by the year 1260 it had become Chianti, following a regular development in Italian phonology that had taken place in the intervening centuries. Chianti has ever since been the name of this lovely wine district of Tuscany between Florence, Siena and Arezzo, and in people's minds the wine it produces has stood for all Italian wine. For centuries the Chianti vineyards belonged to rich Florentine merchant families who took much more interest in their vineyards than the old feudal nobility elsewhere in Italy: wine is after all a trading commodity and merchants have never looked down on the patient toil involved in it. This would seem to be the reason why Chianti has always been a wine of quality, made and looked after with more seriousness than other Italian wines, and why the area strictly entitled to use the name is clearly defined – for many centuries by tradition and since 1932 by law. The area delimited is that of the Chianti classico, the three communes of the old Chianti League and a few other districts where the soil has the same composition. This classical Chianti can be recognized by the black crowing cock on the neck of the bottle. Although some white wine is produced here and there, Chianti should be red, a clear light red due to the combination of two types of black grapes (Sangiovese and Canaiolo) and one white (Trebbiano). In old-fashioned Chianti vineyards these three vines grow in comradely style supported by a single tree.

However, growers in this old, tradition-steeped wine district are increasingly tending to reorganize their vineyards and plant them in the French manner – meaning that picturesqueness may be lost but quality gained. The wine that most people know as Chianti, light, fresh and with a pleasant aroma of flowers, in graceful straw-encased bottles,

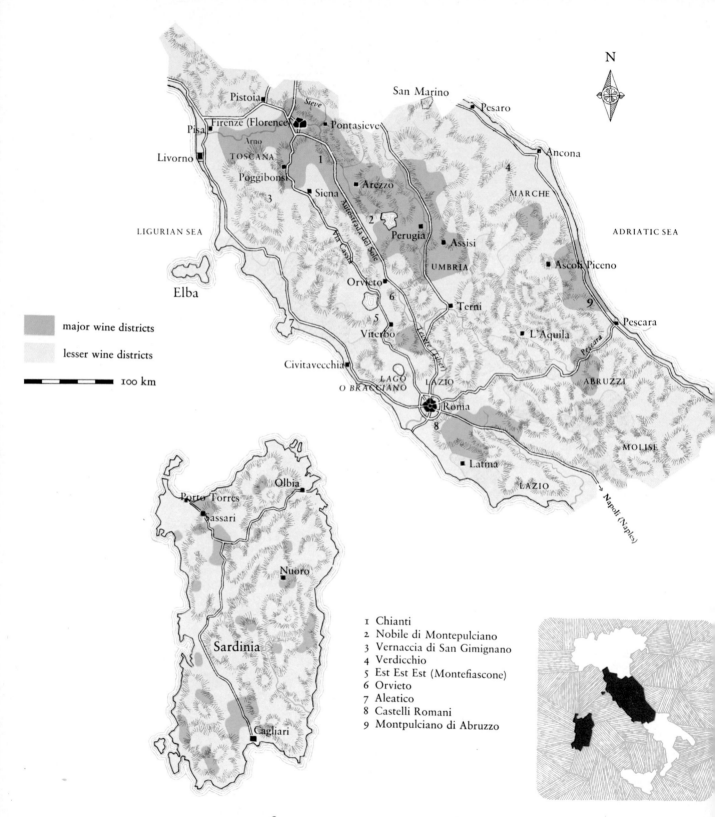

N

San Marino
Pesaro
Ancona
MARCHE

Pistoia
Sieve
Firenze (Florence)
Pontasieve
Pisa
Arno
Livorno
TOSCANA
1
Poggibonsi
Siena
Arezzo
2
Via Cassia
Autostrada del Sole
Perugia
Assisi
UMBRIA
Ascoli Piceno

LIGURIAN SEA

ADRIATIC SEA

Elba

major wine districts

lesser wine districts

100 km

3

Orvieto
6
5
Viterbo
Terni
9
L'Aquila
Pescara
Pescara

7

Civitavecchia
LAGO O BRACCIANO
LAZIO
Via Cassia
ABRUZZI

Roma
8

MOLISE

Latina
LAZIO

Napoli (Naples)

Olbia
Porto Torres
Sassari

Nuoro

Sardinia

Cagliari

1 Chianti
2 Nobile di Montepulciano
3 Vernaccia di San Gimignano
4 Verdicchio
5 Est Est Est (Montefiascone)
6 Orvieto
7 Aleatico
8 Castelli Romani
9 Montpulciano di Abruzzo

old Chianti vineyards different varieties vine may cling to the same tree for support

s the simplest sort, unpretentious and ntended for drinking young; the Chianti of small Italian restaurants he world over. In good Florentine nd Sienese restaurants, however, you re served a different Chianti in onventional bottles. It is a deep pomegranate red, of a fiery disposition, wine that has to age for eight years, therwise it is too harsh. It can be a very fine wine, rounded and distinguished, well balanced and with an enchanting violet bouquet.

Near the hill town of San Gimignano, recognizable from afar by its many towers, there grows the only outstanding white wine of Tuscany, he Vernaccia di San Gimignano, which is dry and soft at the same time, and was much liked by Michelangelo. South of the Arno is the old country of the Etruscans; vineyards still surround the tombs of these first wine growers of Italy. The best wine of this region is Orvieto, a white wine grown on volcanic tuff. It derives ts characteristic freshness of taste, ts gentle hint of bitterness and its subtle bouquet from the deep cellars in the tuff where it ferments under a blanket of silky white moulds. The sweet Orvieto Abboccato, sweetened by the addition of the juice of shrivelled grapes during its fermentation in the cask, is generally regarded as the best wine of this Umbrian district;

unjustly in the opinion of the writer – a dry Orvieto is at least as good, a fine wine and one of the best in Italy. Just south of Orvieto, on Lake Bolsena near Montefiascone, grows the famed Est Est Est, the wine that caused Bishop Fugger to forget his arranged meeting with the Pope in 1111. The bishop was travelling from Augsburg to Rome. As he was something of a gastronome and wanted to run no risks, he sent his manservant on ahead each day to secure rooms at the inn with the best wine. The servant indicated the inn by chalking the Latin word *Est!* (Here it is) on the door. When the German bishop rode into Montefiascone he saw the words Est! Est!! Est!!! scrawled on an inn door, so delighted was the servant with its wine. The bishop shared his servant's enthusiasm, forgot Rome and the Pope, and stayed in Montefiascone. He lies buried in the Romanesque

church against the hill. On his gravestone his servant recorded that his master rests there eternally for having liked Est Est Est too much.

The wine of Rome is the wine of the Alban hills. This is where Romans go in summer weekends to escape the oppressive heat of the Eternal City and eat magnificent fare at outdoor restaurants, seated at long tables under the chestnut trees, drinking the gold-coloured wine which is grown behind the inns. Or they buy a piece of roast sucking pig on the way and then perch on rickety chairs in front of dark little wineries where a signboard announces that wine is served from the cask. In all those enchanting small towns and villages of the Alban hills, in Frascati, Grottaferrata, Marino, Velletri, the sun gleams on carafes of blond wine that is fruity and young, has a little bite to it and a suggestion of volcanic bitterness.

Southern Italy and Sicily

A wine grows in the plain north of Naples that has been famed since classical Antiquity; its praises were sung by the Roman poet Horace. This is Falerno (ancient Falernum), and the best is the white, which comes just short of being absolutely dry and has a singular fragrance probably due to the fact – rare in a white wine – that the crushed grapes are left to ferment with their skins before being pressed.

On the eastern flanks of smoking Vesuvius grows the best-known Neapolitan wine, the Lacrima Christi. The ancestral vine is said to have sprung up at the spot where Christ sat looking out over the Bay of Naples in all its beauty and wept bitter tears when He saw that even this piece of earthly paradise had been spoiled by human wickedness. The true Lacrima Christi is a dry white wine with just a hint of sweetness lurking in it and the slightly bitter aftertaste characteristic of wines from volcanic soil. Volcanic soil is probably also the explanation of its remarkable and intriguing aroma. It is an excellent wine to accompany all those splendid seafood dishes of small octopus, crabs, and shellfish that Neapolitan cooks work such wonders with. Unfortunately the evocative name of this wine has proved rather too much of a temptation: in Naples all sorts of sweet white wines, undistinguished rosés, and even ordinary reds are sold as Lacrima Christi. There is a sweet variety, the Lacrima Christi Liquoroso, made from shrivelled grapes, but it is difficult to come by a genuine example of it.

There are many wines from the heel and toe of the Italian 'boot' that taste excellent when drunk locally, especially the Apulian wines, but they are never met with outside of Italy.

It was in Sicily that Odysseus gave the one-eyed Polyphemus good Greek wine to drink; maybe this was the start of wine growing on this hot island with its loose volcanic soil. At the extreme corner of the island, from where Africa can be seen on a clear day, lies the old port of Marsala, the *Marsh-el-Allah*, 'Haven of God', of the Arabs. Here a heavy, brownish-red wine is made by taking cooked must (this accounts for the resulting caramel flavour) and wine fortified by alcohol, and blending it with the strong white wine of the district. (There is an old Sicilian tradition of drinking wine mixed with cooked must on the feast of Santa Lucia.) A good Marsala can be an excellent wine that at its best

Sicilian vineyards with Etna in the background

moments invites comparison with a Madeira. Probably it is the volcanic soil that gives both wines their slightly bitter aftertaste. Nelson, whose fleet used the harbour of Marsala, had a great liking for Marsala and used to serve it to his officers. Marsala in fact was developed by the Englishmen Woodhouse and Ingham the latter had experience of supplying wine to the Royal Navy. When Garibaldi and his thousand men landed in Sicily in 1860 he served all of his heroes with a good glass of Marsala before battle, with obviously good results. One type of Marsala is still called Garibaldi dolce, 'Sweet Garibaldi'. Like Madeira, Marsala can achieve a venerable age. Marsalas dating from 1838 can taste as fresh as if they were only ten years old.

Marsala is one of those wines that is not always left as it is and is blended with eggs, the famous Marsala al' uovo, with milk of almonds, or even with chocolate or coffee.

Sicily also offers outstanding table wines, red and white Corvo from the Palermo district, the red Faro from around Messina and the white and red wines from the slopes of Mount Etna. The best Malvasia – a very sweet dessert wine – of the whole of the Mediterranean basin is Malvasia di Lipari, which comes from the little volcanic islands of Lipari, Stromboli and Salina north of Sicily.

1 Falerno
2 Lacrima Christi
3 Malvasia
4 Etna
5 Corvo
6 Alcamo
7 Pachino
8 Faro
9 Marsala

major wine districts

lesser wine districts

100 km

Switzerland

Vineyards by the Lake of Geneva

The finest compliment ever paid to Swiss wines came from the gastronomer and philosopher Brillat-Savarin; unfortunately it sounds today like a banal advertising slogan. He said that they were 'fresh and clear as a mountain stream'. He was referring of course to the Swiss white wines which do possess those fresh, cool and limpid qualities that bring mountain air and babbling streams to mind. Switzerland produces more white than red wine, and the whites are better than the reds, with one exception. The red wines of Ticino, in the sunny south of the country, which are drunk straight from the cellar and accompany the markedly Italian-influenced cuisine of this beautiful region, are exceedingly pleasant. But away from their native districts they would quickly lose their charm. The best, and best-known, Swiss wines come from the country around Lake Neuchâtel, from the northern shores of the Lake of Geneva (Lake Léman) and from the Rhône valley about Sion and Martigny.

The white wines of Neuchâtel are dry and light. The chalky soil gives them a natural tendency to sparkle, and this is exploited. Excellent *vins mousseux* are made at Neuchâtel by the *méthode champenoise*: light and dry, and wonderfully fresh.

The north shore of the Lake of Geneva enjoys both direct sunlight, of a Mediterranean intensity here, and its myriad reflections from the lake. Fine wines grow on these warm slopes on either side of Lausanne; in the opinion of many they are the best wines in all Switzerland. They are dry, fragrant and agreeable, especially those from La Côte and Lavaux. The famous Swiss non-alcoholic grape juice also comes from these same vineyards.

wine-growing areas

30 km

The young Rhône splashes down from its source in a glacial cave to the Lake of Geneva, seeking its way among the mountains, and along its banks grow the best-known Swiss wines. There is for example the white, jolly Fendant, always served poured out from high above the glass to make it sparkle. Fendant is made from Chasselas grapes, the thin skins of which burst (*fendre*) when they are fully ripe. The seeds are supposed to have been brought to Switzerland in the knapsacks of Swiss mercenaries returning from Fontainebleau, where Chasselas vines grew in the gardens. Clear, dry and light, Fendant is well-matched with fondue. Johannisberg comes from Sylvaner grapes introduced from Germany; it is a gentle, sweet wine, dubbed a 'ladies' wine' in Switzerland. It tastes absolutely delicious with asparagus and ham.

One of the best, if not the best, of Swiss red wines comes from the Dôle area. It is made from Gamay grapes, also said to have been taken there by homebound soldiers. In Valais you may, if you are lucky, have the opportunity of tasting the extremely rare glacier wine. This is white wine taken when only a few weeks old up to little wooden 'cellars' on the edges of the glaciers to mature in the invigorating mountain cold. It is a remarkable wine, absolutely dry with a strange bitterness in its aftertaste; it bites the tongue and is headier than might be supposed of anything so dry and fresh.

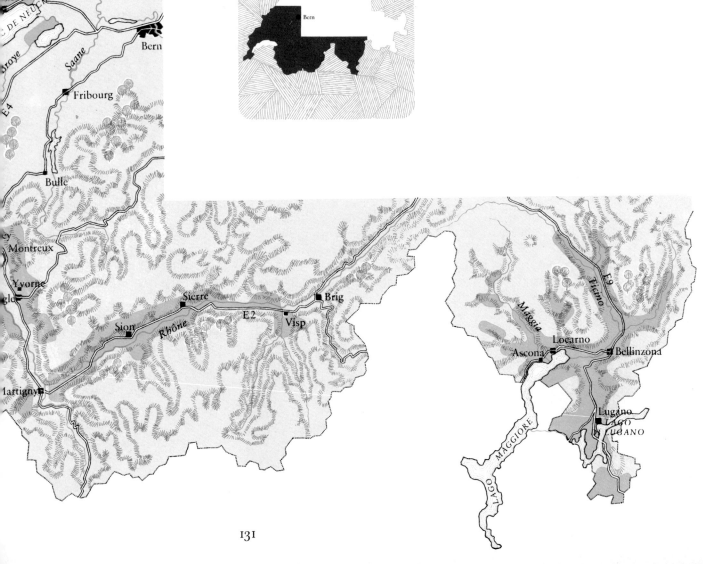

Austria

Like Switzerland, Austria is preeminently a country of white wines. There are ordinary, everyday table wines from the Tyrol, but also wines of good quality from the Wachau and the countryside around Vienna.

In the Wachau the Danube flows between steep green banks, the light green of vineyards and apricot orchards below surmounted by the darker green of firwoods. Above it all rise the ruins of medieval fortresses. There are toy villages with frivolous rococo churches and everywhere there are friendly inns where the light-gold Wachau wine is served in wide rummers. The grapes that grow here on the trellised vines are the Rhine Riesling – this is a true Austrian grape variety, despite the name – and the Austrian Grüner Veltliner. The best-known Wachau wines come from Krems, Dürnstein and Spitz; the best are probably those from Krems. All the wines of the Wachau are of a beautiful, lustrous gold, fragrant, fresh, enchanting and of a gentle roundness. Wine growing here must be an ancient occupation; this is one of the few districts where it dates from Celtic times – apparently from as early as 400 BC.

The famous wine villages of Grinzing, Nussdorf, Heiligenstadt, Sievering and the Kahlenberg, are situated in the immediate environs of Vienna. This is not a country of great wines; these are the villages where you go in the evenings to drink the Heurige at the houses of growers who have *ausg'steckt*. This means that they have put out of their windows a bunch of fir branches on a stick to announce that they serve Heurige from the cask, wine from the most recent vintage. It is drunk with roast chicken to the sound of music from a four-piece tavern band, the Viennese *Schrammelmusik*, out of doors at long tables in summer, indoors under the low, beamed ceilings by the tiled stoves in winter. Schubert and Beethoven were here before you to sample the Heurige.

South of Vienna lies another small wine village, Gumpoldskirchen, where one of the finest Austrian wines is grown: the wine drunk at the Congress of Vienna in 1814; the wine that sparkled under the chandeliers at Schönbrunn. It is a deep-gold, lustrous, mellow wine, surprisingly fragrant. It is a wine that seems to go with three-four time and can be very treacherous.

In Burgenland, by the Neusiedlersee, where the summers are hot and the autumns long and warm, there are grown, besides some rather heady white wines, the best of the Austrian red wines. Made from a variety of grape called Blaufränkisch, it is full-bodied and rather heavy. The old free town of Rust also lies near the lake. Storks nest on the roofs of the houses and the climate is so favourable that the grapes are visited by the *Botrytis cinerea*. This makes possible the harvesting of selected shrivelled grapes – *Trockenbeerenauslese*. The result, Ruster Ausbruch, was a favourite wine of Goethe and Bismarck.

All Austrian wines carry the seal *Wein aus Österreich*. Wines from Burgenland, Lower Austria (Wachau), Styria and Vienna are entitled to be labelled with their place of origin.

CZECHOSLOVAKIA

Haugsdorf

Poysdorf

March (Morava)

E84

Langenlois

Dürnstein   Krems

Spitz

Loiben

Klosterneuburg   Vienna

St. Pölten

E5

Danube

Gumpoldskirchen

Baden

Leitha

Neusiedl

Eisenstadt   Oggau

Wiener Neustadt   St. Margarethen   Rust

Mattersburg   NEUSIEDLER SEE

white wines

red and white wines

50 km

HUNGARY

E7

Bruck a. d. Mur

N

Graz

Raab

E93

Leibnitz   Klöch

Mur

YUGOSLAVIA

Hungary

When in the ninth century AD the Magyars galloped westwards out of the Asiatic steppes and through the Carpathian passes to descend on the Hungarian plain, a mysterious people from the Caucasus rode with them; the latter had been wine growers from time immemorial. In the new homeland they found sunshine, fertile soil and the neglected vineyards left behind by the Romans, and so they resumed their old craft. Hungary has ever since been a country of excellent wines honestly made, wines full of character and mettle. On the northern shore of Lake Balaton, on the slopes of old volcanoes, the rich wines of Badacsony and Balatonfüred grow in a soil of weathered basalt and ancient alluvial sands.

The golden-yellow Szürkebarát ('Grey Friar' – so-called from the Pinot Gris grape) is a fiery, dry,

flower-scented Riesling (Rizling) that flows so satin-smooth over the tongue that its potency is only noticed when it is too late. Kéknyelü is a fine, green-gold wine with a spicy aroma; its name means 'Blue Stalk', after the Blaustengler grape. According to the cellarers of Balaton, these two wines should be drunk from as big a glass as possible – so that the drinker's nose goes into the glass enabling taste and smell to be enjoyed simultaneously.

Good white table wines come from northern Hungary, such as the mellow Ezerjó from Mor (the name means 'thousand times good' and the grape it is made from is an ancient Hungarian variety)), and the dry Léanyka (also named after its grape, literally 'Young Girl'). Eger, a snug, gold-yellow little Baroque town, also in the north of the country, is famous for its Egri Bikavér, 'Bull's Blood', a deep-red, fiery and lustrous wine, smelling of pinks and vanilla. It is matured in the deep cellars dug out

by French prisoners of war in the seventeenth century. It derives its deep colour from the dark skins of the Kadarka grape which are left to ferment for some considerable time in the vats with the must; the popular name is entirely fanciful.

In eastern Hungary, among low, vine-clad hills, lies Tokay, where one of the world's great wines is matured. Everywhere in these hills are to be seen cellar entrances so low that you have to lower your head to enter. They were deliberately made like this, it is said, so that everyone should bow before this magnificent wine. There are several types of Tokay: the commonest sort is the Furmint, a spicy, sweet, blond wine. Then there is Tokaji Szamarodni (the qualifying word is actually Polish and means 'naturally grown' or 'as it comes'), a beautiful gold wine from bunches that contain both normally ripe and overripe grapes. There is a sweet and a dry variety, according to the proportion

Wine cellars

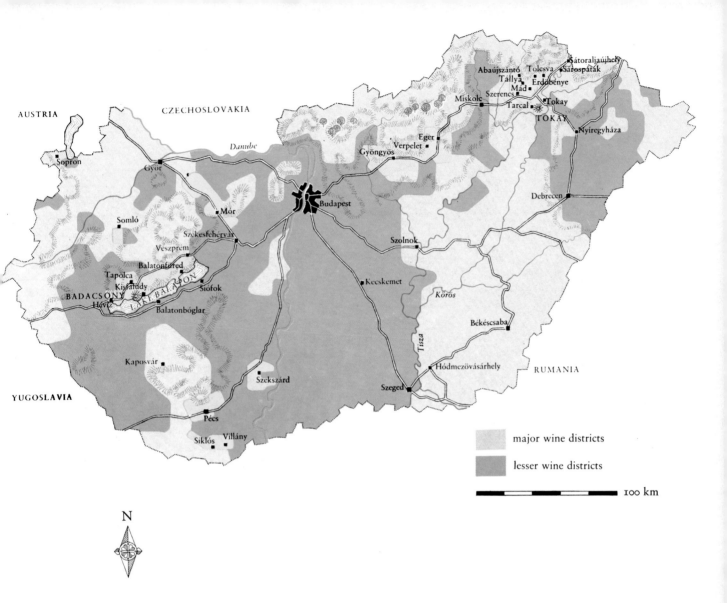

major wine districts

lesser wine districts

100 km

N

of overripe grapes in the bunch. A dry Szamarodni has a racy, full-flavoured quality that makes it an excellent apéritif. Finally there is the 'king of wines and the wine of kings', as Louis XIV, who was very fond of this wine, is said to have called Tokaji Aszu. It is a glowing, golden brown and has the fragrance of concentrated essence of wine. To produce this celestial wine, the grapes are left on the vine at least to November, until they are greyed and shrivelled from the *pourriture noble*, the *Botrytis cinerea*. These selected grapes (*aszu* means selected) are pressed in very small quantities over long periods of time. This was formerly done by bare feet in small tubs, but today specially constructed machines knead the grapes until a smooth 'dough' or paste is produced. This is then added to ordinary must. For very expensive Tokay, five *puttonyos*, a measure of about 6 gallons, are added to a 35-gallon *göncz*. Three or four *puttonyos* to a cask is the most usual ratio; six is very exceptional. The number of *puttonyos* is stated on the label of a Tokaji Aszu. This mixture is then fermented very slowly to produce Tokay. Attracted by its glorious golden colour, the medieval alchemist Paracelsus travelled to Tokay hoping to be able to make gold out of the wine. The flowery aroma and honey sweetness of Tokay make it a superb dessert wine, a fragrant delight to follow good food.

Yugoslavia, Greece, Bulgaria, Rumania and the Soviet Union

YUGOSLAVIA

As you travel from north to south in Yugoslavia you make the transition from central Europe to the Balkans, from little towns and villages with a slightly marzipan, Austrian character to the more highly seasoned Turkish atmosphere of Bosnia and Macedonia, and a parallel change can be discerned in the country's wines. The wines of northern Yugoslavia, especially those of Slovenia, are typically central European. They come in the slender bottles familiar in Germany and Austria, and the most commonly used grapes are the Riesling, Sylvaner and Traminer. The quality of these Slovenian wines can be excellent, particularly if they hail from the country around Ljutomer and Maribor. Here you find fresh, agreeable and fruity white wines, dry or nearly dry, and well worth their modest prices. Ljutomer also produces a heavy, sweet white wine from late-picked grapes (the German term *Spätlese* appears on the label); it is much prized by the Yugoslavs who call it Tigrovo Mleko, 'Tiger-milk', because of its fiery character.

The best-known Yugoslav red wine is Prokupac from Serbia (there is also a rosé). It is produced by a vine that has grown in Yugoslav soil for centuries; a robust, rather emphatic red wine, it is unexpectedly fruity if you get one of good quality. It is ideal for barbecues, tasting good with any charcoal-grilled food.

The hot valley of the Neretva, in the neighbourhood of the picturesque little town of Mostar is the home of one of the best Yugoslav wines, the white Žilavka, made from ancient native Yugoslav grapes. It is a dry wine, but so rich and well defined in taste that it often gives an impression of sweetness. Its high alcoholic strength makes it treacherously heady.

Along the Dalmatian coast they make the very sweet, golden-brown Prosek from grapes which have been sun-dried into raisins.

GREECE

Regrettably little is left of the reputation Greece enjoyed in classical

PRODUCT OF YUGOSLAVIA

PROKUPAC

IVEX

RED TABLE WINE

Prokupac is a Serbian red table wine. The grapes are cultivated in winegrowing areas along Morava river, and its tradition dating back to the earliest times.

Alcohol by Volume 12%

ISTRAVINOEXPORT, RIJEKA

ΜΠΩΜΕ 7   ΟΙΝ/ΜΑ 16

ORIGINAL WINE OF PATRAS

Mavrodaphne

Fine RED Wine

Produced and Bottled by
-PATRAIKI-

UNION OF AGRICULTURAL CO-OPERATIVES

ΕΝΩΣΙΣ ΓΕΩΡΓΙΚΩΝ ΣΥΝΕΤΑΙΡΙΣΜΩΝ ΠΑΤΡΩΝ
ALK. GEH. 14-16%
PRODUCE OF GREECE

ΒΑΡ. ΚΑΘ. 720 ΓΡΑΜ.   ΑΡ. ΑΔ. 4/10-11-1964
ΕΛΛ. ΠΡΟΙΟΝ

Bulgarian viticulture was neglected for centuries. Today, however, wine is the concern of the state, like everything else in Bulgaria. There are enormous cooperative wineries and laboratories directed by university-trained oenologists, and although the wines produced may not be great, they are very drinkable. Examples are the fragrant, dry white Misket Karlovo (Child of the Valley of Roses) and Dimiat, also white, made from the grape of that name. Hemus is a sweet white wine. Cabernet is made from French grapes of that name. The red wine that is best liked in Bulgaria itself is the fairly heavy, dark Mavrud from Thrace and the Rhodope.

Perhaps in an effort to make things easy for the many German tourists who visit the Black Sea coast, the Bulgarians market all kinds of wine of generally unspecified origin under romantic names like Klosterkeller and Donau Perle.

times as a land of great wines. A vast amount of wine is produced in Greece, but by far the greater part of it is ordinary and anonymous, drunk in the local tavernas and by the Greeks in their homes. The most characteristic is retsina – a very light white wine, usually not more than 9%, absolutely dry and flavoured with resin. The biting taste of turpentine is not generally appreciated by non-Greeks, at least not at first, but beginners quickly grow accustomed to it. It must be said that it suits the Greek climate perfectly and goes well with grilled fish or lamb shish kebabs, those two simple but tasty pillars of Greek cooking. The tradition of resinating wine is very ancient (see page 29). The best retsina still comes from Attica, as it did 2,500 years ago. One of the best unresinated Greek wines comes from Archanes in Crete: an unpretentious but acceptable red, and also white, table wine. It makes an excellent wine for every day.

Before World War II the sweet, golden-brown Samos, from the beautiful, flower-scented island of that name near the Turkish coast, had a measure of popularity outside Greece. This is a muscatel; its fermentation is stopped at an early stage by the addition of pure wine alcohol, so it has a high sugar content.

Sweet Samos has gone out of fashion, but perhaps one day the wine

cooperative on the island might consider exporting the dry white Samos. It is virtually never seen except on the island but it is an exceptionally pleasant, fragrant and spicy wine which could compete successfully with cheap German and Spanish white wines. Mavrodaphne is a heavy, sweet red wine from Patras in the Peloponnesus. It suggests, remotely, a ruby port and, like the sweet wines of southern France, it has to mature for several years in casks left in the open air.

BULGARIA

Bulgaria is supposed to be a very ancient wineland. According to one version of the myth the Greek wine god Dionysus came from the Rhodope mountains in the south of the country. For those who prefer to stick to demonstrable facts, the museum at Plovdiv (ancient Philippopolis) has a collection of impressive and beautifully worked gold beakers and tankards from which Thracians, ancestors of the present Bulgarians, drank wine centuries before the present era. Occupation by Turks, which Bulgaria experienced from the fourteenth to the nineteenth century, did wine growing little good. The Turks, being Muslims, preferred to cultivate roses for perfume and tobacco for cigarettes, so

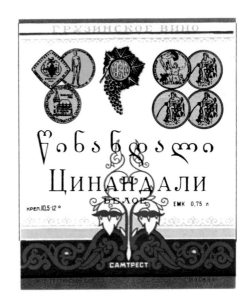

RUMANIA

When Trajan's legions conquered Dacia for Rome in the first century AD they found a wine-drinking people who once even took up arms in defence of their vines when the priests wanted to uproot them. From an early date a couple of sweet dessert wines of excellent quality have been made in Rumania: the golden-brown spicy Murfatlar from Dobrudja and the lustrous gold Cotnari from Moldavia, which before World War I was even served in big Parisian restaurants. Today both types go principally to East Germany and the Soviet Union, where Cotnari is *the* wine for official banquets in the Kremlin. Rumanians have set about improving their viticulture in an energetic and scientific manner. The area of cultivation has been increased by about 50% and foreign vines have been successfully introduced. The peasant farmers themselves have continued to produce wine for their own use. The best Rumanian wines are grown in the old vineyards belonging to the Patriarchate – but these are not for sale. In recent years Rumania has exported many pleasant, carefully produced wines at reasonable prices, such as the Fetească regală (the 'maiden's grape' that also grows in Hungary) and the Traminer from Transylvania. From the same region comes the fragrant, rather mellower Furmint Zagar; and then there are the rounded, gentle red wines of Oltenia such as Cabernet Sîmburesti and the Negru Vîrtos, the latter from an ancient indigenous type of grape.

THE SOVIET UNION

Soviet wines are seldom found in the West. Russians are sweet-toothed and

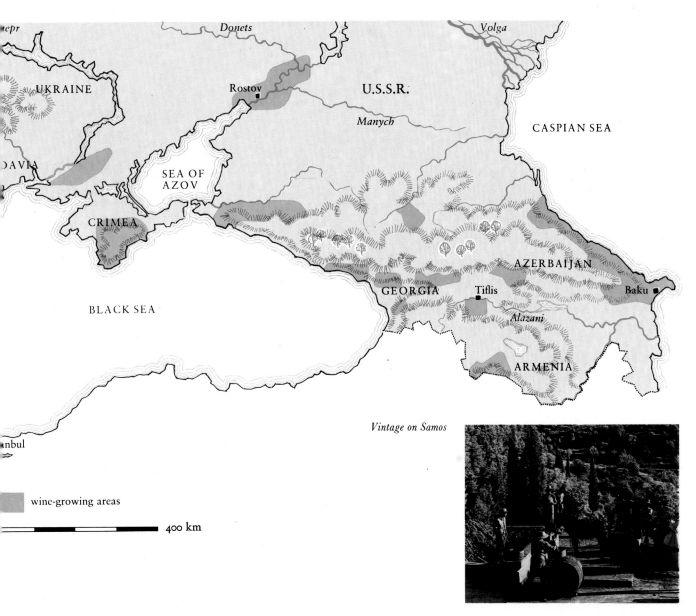

UKRAINE

Donets

Volga

Rostov

U.S.S.R.

Manych

CASPIAN SEA

OAVIA

SEA OF
AZOV

CRIMEA

AZERBAIJAN

GEORGIA   Tiflis

Baku

BLACK SEA

Alazani

ARMENIA

Vintage on Samos

nbul

wine-growing areas

400 km

their wines are mostly too sweet for Western liking.

However, there are some agreeable wines produced in Russia, especially in the very old wine districts of the Caucasus; the best of all are from Georgia. Sparkling wine is made around Rostov on the Don – again it is much too sweet for Western tastes. Intensive experiments are being conducted with French grapes, particularly in Moldavia, the territory that was Rumanian before World War II. The Russians also make other rather sweet wines that they call port, sherry or Madeira to taste, but these bear little resemblance to their originals. Efforts are being made to turn the Crimea, with its excellent climate, into a region for the production of high-class wines, using foreign grapes such as Riesling, Sylvaner, Aligoté and Pinot Gris, apparently not without success.

North and South Africa

Vineyards near Stellenbosch, South Africa

NORTH AFRICA

North Africa is in a sense a very recent. but also a very ancient wine country. In Egypt the pharaohs were drinking wine in about 3000 BC. When the Phoenicians founded Carthage in 814 BC they planted vines (Carthaginian wines were famed in antiquity); and when the Romans conquered North Africa they found wine made there, the wine Cleopatra spiced by dissolving her pearls in it. The Arab conquest meant the end of viticulture – Muslims may not drink alcohol – but with the coming of the French at the end of the nineteenth and the beginning of the twentieth century the vine returned in glory. North Africa at present accounts for about one tenth of total world wine production. This wine is not drunk locally – the people are still Muslim – and most of it is exported. Formerly it disappeared anonymously in all the small Midi wines, to give them colour and body. But now these wines of the Midi are so improved in quality that they no longer need that dash of dark Algerian wine. Thus North African wines have the chance they undoubtedly merit of an independent life. Excellent red wines come from Algeria, especially from the uplands around Mascara, Zaccar and Tlemcen. Twelve of them are even entitled to a

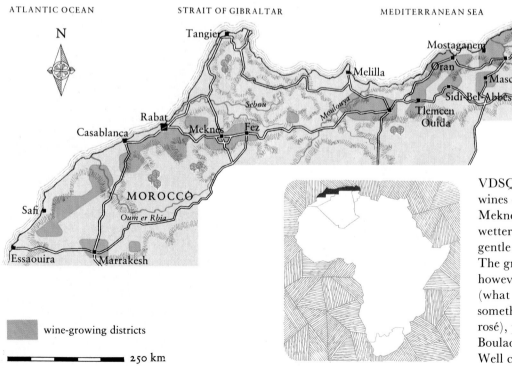

VDSQ *appellation*. The best Moroccan wines come from the region around Meknes and Fez, where the climate is wetter than in the rest of the country: gentle red wines, pleasant to drink. The great speciality of Morocco, however, is a very light-coloured rosé (what is termed a *vin gris* in France, something between a white and a rosé), particularly the one from Boulaouane, south of Casablanca. Well chilled, this is a splendid summer

wine-growing districts

250 km

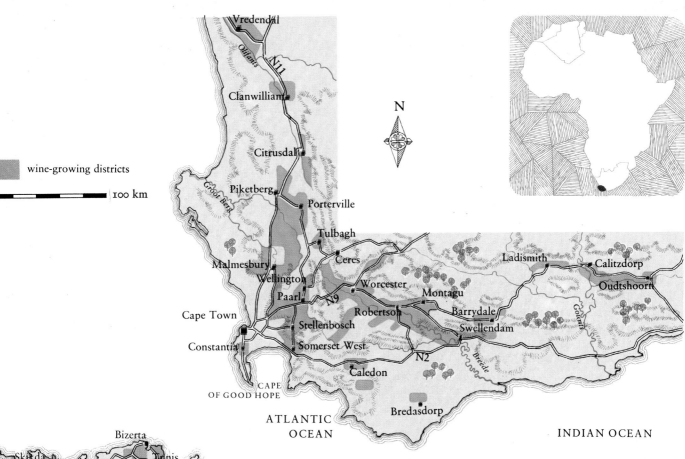

wine-growing districts

100 km

N

TUNISIA

SOUTH AFRICA

The vineyards of South Africa are situated near the Cape and across the mountains in the Little Karoo. The Cape vineyards were founded in the seventeenth century, for the most part by French Huguenots who had fled there from the persecutions that followed the revocation of the Edict of Nantes, and had been hospitably received by Jan van Riebeeck, leader of the first Dutch settlers. These vineyards are still among the best in South Africa. It is a beautiful region with a delightful climate and many fine old estates. A good number of them date from the seventeenth century and you can see gables like those along the Amsterdam canals, but on elegant white villas. Dutch

names appear frequently on South African wine labels: those of places such as Stellenbosch, Paarl and Franschhoek (the last a reminder of the Huguenots), and of estates like Theuniskraal, Oude Molen and Nederburg. One Cape wine attained world renown in the last century: the sweet golden-brown Constantia, served at the tables of Queen Victoria, Kaiser Wilhelm and other exalted persons. In the Netherlands the sweet red Cape Springbok used to be favoured, especially as a medicinal wine.

All the vines of the Cape were of course imported from Europe – Riesling and Cabernet, for example, and even the Spanish Palomino, from which a sherry of reasonable quality is made, popular in Britain.

wine, absolutely dry, fresh and lustrous. Tunisia too produces good, full red wines and a sweet muscatel of some worth. The white wines of these regions all suffer from a lack of acidity and do not equal the reds in quality. Egypt too has taken up viticulture again. Egyptian wines with evocative names like Queen Cleopatra and Omar Khayyam are making their appearance, chiefly in hotels along the Nile.

Israel, Cyprus and Lebanon

ISRAEL

The wines of Israel, Cyprus and the Lebanon are Biblical wines, for the ancient Israelites drank not only the wines of their own Promised Land, but others from Cyprus and the Lebanon. Wine is mentioned some hundreds of times in the Bible. It must have permeated the whole of life and thought in ancient Israel. The old Biblical vineyards largely disappeared after the Saracens and later the Turks conquered the Holy Land. This did not mean the end of wine altogether, for Crusaders' tales make it clear that wine was certainly still made, including a famous one called Blood of Judas. Unfortunately we no longer known precisely where it came from.

In the nineteenth century Baron Edmond de Rothschild gave Palestine vineyards once more, vast estates near Rishon-le-Zion south of Tel Aviv, and Zikhron Ya'aqov north of that port. Vines were brought from southern France, notably the Grenache for red wines and Semillon and Clairette for white, and courageously the ancient crafts of viticulture were resumed. And not without success – although the country's summers are too hot for the production of wines of outstanding quality. Israeli wine is always on the heavy side and strongly emphasized in taste. This is not necessarily a bad fault in red wines – there are very acceptable Israeli table wines, such as the Carmel, for example – but the whites have insufficient acidity. White wines are made into *vins mousseux*, also sweet, and to cater for the fashion for rosé a semi-sweet wine of this type is produced.

CYPRUS

No one knows how old the viticulture of Cyprus is, but Solomon drank Cypriot wine with the Queen of Sheba in about 1000 BC. This may have been the heavy, sweet Commandaria that grows on the slopes of the Troodos mountains north of Limassol and is still famous. True Commandaria, as distinct from the rather mass-produced variety from the big wine 'factories', comes from two villages, Zoopiyi ('life-giving spring') and Kalokhorion ('beautiful village'). The grapes are left to dry for five to six days in the sun, then they are put to ferment in the enormous stone vats that can be seen at the back of many houses in the villages. Afterwards the wine matures in small, hermetically sealed casks, preferably for several years – five, six or even eight – and then maturation in the bottle follows. During this time it becomes golden brown, syrupy, a concentrated essence of wine. The Crusaders who, led by Richard Lionheart, conquered Cyprus in the twelfth century took immediate possession of the Commandaria vineyards. When the wine began to arrive in western Europe it attracted a good deal of notice. It became the wine of the English monarchs until well into the seventeenth century. Besides the exceptionally sweet Commandaria, a number of red and white wines of reasonable quality grow in Cyprus and are sold under such splendidly romantic names as Coeur de Lion, Othello (in

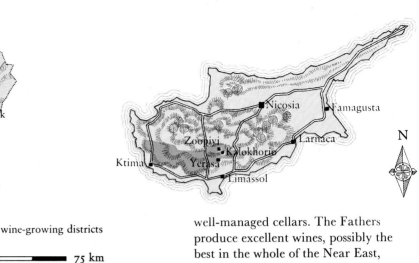

wine-growing districts

75 km

well-managed cellars. The Fathers
produce excellent wines, possibly the
best in the whole of the Near East,
from French vines imported before the
phylloxera disaster. These were chiefly
the Grenache, Merlot and Clairette,
but there were also ancient indigenous
vines and even the Hungarian
Kadarka. In this area too the white
wines suffer from a lack of acid, but
the red table wines are excellent and
for ten years now a pleasant light
rosé has had much success. Ksará
wines are well made. constitutionally
strong, and can tolerate even tropical
heat without harm. A lot of Ksará
wine is therefore exported to Africa
for the luxury hotels springing up
there, and for European embassies.

Shakespeare's play, it will be
remembered, he was governor of
Cyprus and strangled Desdemona in
the castle at Famagusta), and
Aphrodite (the goddess of love was
born of the sea foam on the southern
shore of the island). A good apéritif
is made by the sherry process; popular
in Britain, it is quite a reasonable
drink, but purists do not accept that
it is a sherry.

LEBANON

Wine from the slopes of Mount
Lebanon was famous 3,000 years ago,
but here too the Saracens and Turks
allowed the vineyards to decay.
However, in 1857 a group of Jesuits
started cultivation on the eastern
slopes of Mount Lebanon and the
fertile Bekáa valley. This is the vast
Ksará vineyard, a model estate with
vines which are tended with true
French care, and with particularly

143

Vintage on Cyprus

Australia

Vines were first planted in Australia at Farm Cove in 1788 by Captain Arthur Phillip, who led the First Fleet of settlers, but it is only since the 1960's that fine table wines have been produced in any quantity. In the past, the taste in Australia was for sweet, heavy wines, high in alcohol, and for fortified wines. Much of the wine production was used for distilling, as it still is, and 1968 was the first year when production of table wines exceeded that of fortified wines. Characteristic Australian products were 'tonic Burgundies' and dessert wines. By 1972 nearly twice as much table wine was made as fortified wine, and this has been made possible in part by the introduction of refrigeration, which enables the wines to mature more slowly and achieve a better balance. Today, the reputation of Australian wines is lower than they deserve, due in part to the fact that they are still marketed under names borrowed from European wines. To call a good Australian wine claret or Chablis does it no credit.

The warm, dry Australian climate is extremely favourable for growing grapes, and naturally makes for full-bodied wines. The soil is rich, but with considerable variation, so that grapes from different parts of the same vineyard can produce both claret-type wines and port-type wines. The wines mature rapidly and are bottled early, fermentation generally taking place in concrete vats. Tartaric acid and tannin are often added to balance the wine.

The area around the Murray River has very low rainfall and the vineyards are irrigated by a series of locks. Mildura, Swan Hill, Corowa and Rutherglen all produce fortified wines, dessert wines and big Burgundies. Dry sherries are the best of the Australian fortified wines, since *flor* is imported from Europe and inoculated into the young wine. The vineyards of Great Western have poorer soil, more suitable for the production of sparkling wines, and the best Australian 'champagne' is made here; the coolness required for secondary fermentation is ensured by long underground galleries known as 'drives'. The best table wines come from the higher, cooler areas, particularly the Hunter River Valley and the vineyards around Adelaide. The red wines from the Hunter River Valley are made mainly from the Cabernet, Syrrah (Shiraz) and Pinot Noir grapes, the Cabernet giving a claret type of wine and the Syrrah, sometimes known as Hermitage, a Rhône type; the white wine, made from Sémillon grapes, is known, confusingly, as Hunter Valley Riesling.

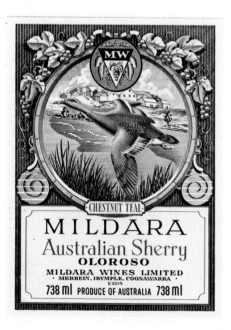

MW

CHESTNUT TEAL

MILDARA
Australian Sherry
OLOROSO
MILDARA WINES LIMITED
· MERBEIN, IRYMPLE, COONAWARRA ·
E2015
738 ml PRODUCE OF AUSTRALIA 738 ml

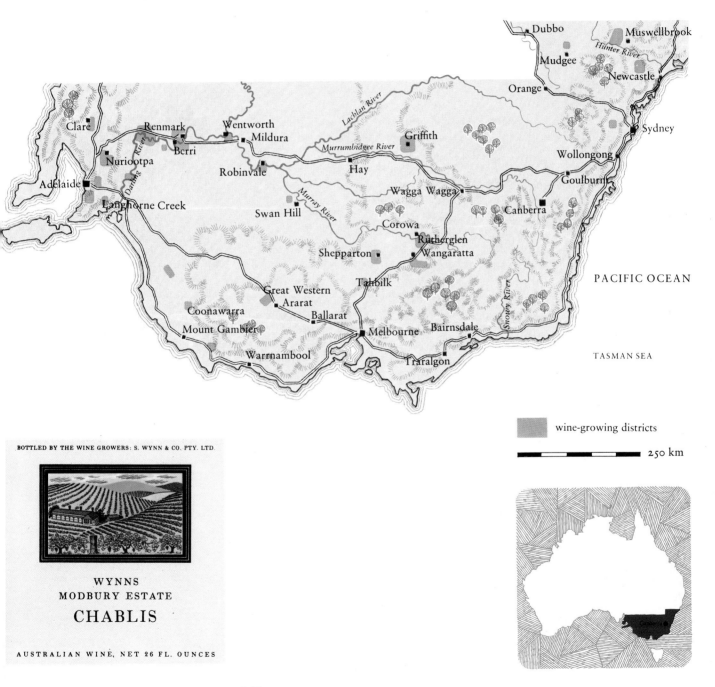

N

PACIFIC OCEAN

TASMAN SEA

Dubbo
Muswellbrook
Hunter River
Mudgee
Newcastle
Orange
Sydney
Clare
Renmark
Wentworth
Mildura
Griffith
Wollongong
Lachlan River
Darling River
Berri
Nuriootpa
Murrumbidgee River
Goulburn
Robinvale
Hay
Adelaide
Wagga Wagga
Canberra
Langhorne Creek
Murray River
Swan Hill
Corowa
Rutherglen
Shepparton
Wangaratta
Great Western
Ararat
Tahbilk
Snowy River
Coonawarra
Ballarat
Bairnsdale
Mount Gambier
Melbourne
Warrnambool
Traralgon

wine-growing districts

250 km

Barossa Valley and Southern Vales

The area around Adelaide produces some of the best Australian wines and is divided into three distinct districts, the Barossa Valley to the north, Southern Vales to the south and Adelaide Metropolitan, close to the city, which is gradually being eroded by urban growth. The main centres are Tanunda, Nurioopta and Angaston in the Barossa Valley, Modbury in Adelaide Metropolitan and Reynella in Southern Vales. Reynella takes its name from John Reynell, who first planted vines here in 1838. Traditionally the Barossa Valley produced apéritif wines, brandies and fortified wines, while the Southern Vales produced red table wines and 'port'. High-quality table wines are now made in both areas.

The red wines from Reynella, made from Cabernet and Syrrah grapes are not labelled 'claret' or 'Burgundy' until the wine has revealed its character, but the Rieslings of the Barossa Valley are genuinely made from the Rhine Riesling grape and German methods are followed closely. Wine-growing in the valley is largely of German origin, started by refugees from religious persecution who settled there in the 1850's, some of whose families are now in their sixth generation as wine-growers. In some years conditions make a *Spätlese* possible, and in individual vineyards the Riesling grapes are left to ripen fully, giving a characteristic strong bouquet. Two of the old wine growing families are the Seppelts, whose main vineyards are at Seppeltsfield, and the Gramps of Orlando. Many of the growers are shareholders in a co-operative, whose main vineyards are at Nurioopta and whose wine is sold under the Kaiserstuhl label.

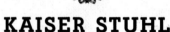

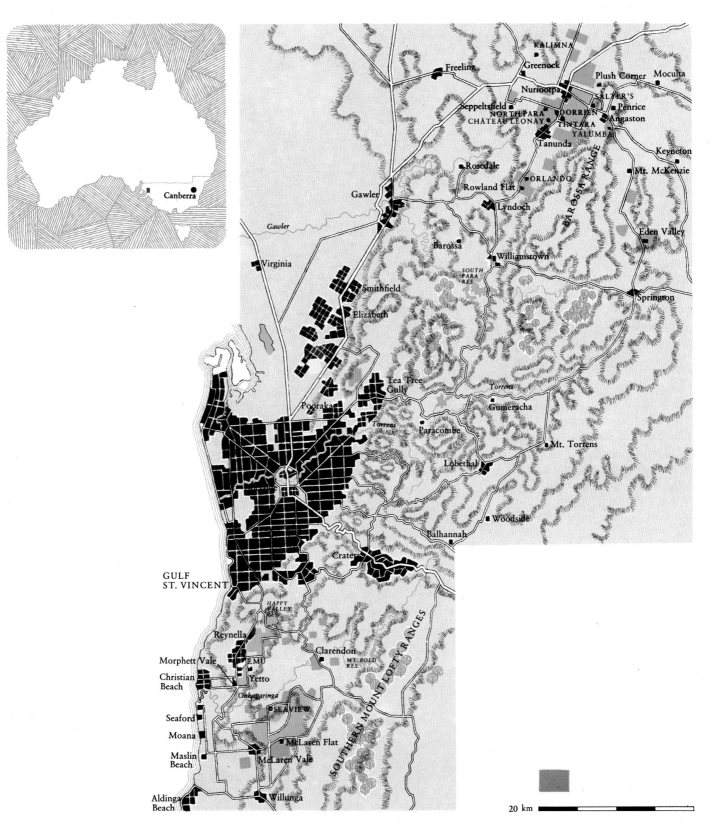

Canberra

Freeling
KALIMNA
Greenock
Plush Corner
Moculta
Nuriootpa
SALTER'S
Seppeltsfield
DORRIEN
Penrice
NORTH PARA
TINTARA
Angaston
CHÂTEAU LEONAY
YALUMBA
Tanunda
Keyneton
Rosedale
Mt. McKenzie
Rowland Flat
ORLANDO
Gawler
Lyndoch
BAROSSA RANGE
Barossa
Eden Valley
Williamstown
Virginia
SOUTH
PARA
RES.
Springton
Smithfield
Elizabeth
Tea Tree
Gully
Poorakar
Torrens
Gumeracha
Torrens
Paracombe
Mt. Torrens
Lobethal
GULF
ST. VINCENT
Woodside
Crater
Balhannah
HAPPY
VALLEY
RES.
Reynella
Clarendon
Morphett Vale
EMU
MT. BOLD
RES.
Christian
Beach
Yetto
SOUTHERN MOUNT LOFTY RANGES
Onkaparinga
Seaford
SEAVIEW
Moana
McLaren Flat
Maslin
Beach
McLaren Vale
Aldinga
Beach
Willunga

20 km

147

North America

According to the saga, when the Vikings made their landfall on the eastern seaboard of North America they found wild vines growing there and consequently they named the country *Vinland*, 'Wineland'. The descendants of the vines they found (probably *vitis labrusca*) still grow in the eastern United States, in the vineyards of Finger Lakes area. The first European vines from *vitis vinifera* were planted in California in the sixteenth century, but the serious establishment of vines there by the Franciscans, who needed them for sacramental wine, dates from the mid-eighteenth century. Descendants of these vines still produce 'Mission grapes'.

Today 400,000 acres in California are under vines, which produce some 2,500,000 tons of grapes a year. As much as half of these are used for the dried fruit industry and much of the wine produced is fortified. The hot California sun often scorches the grapes, and this flavour is less noticeable in fortified wines. California produces three times as much 'sherry' as is made in Spain and ten times as much 'port' as is made in Portugal.

Ninety per cent of American wines are now made in California, but in the nineteenth century the picture was very different, and the main development came in the east, where German immigrants tried to make a new Rhineland on the Ohio river. Very little is left of their vineyards today, and the main production in the eastern United States is in the Finger Lakes area. *Vitis vinifera* has a struggle to survive in the long, very cold winters and the short summers, and the vines grown are mostly hybrids of *vitis labrusca*. Their grapes have a distinctive flavour, generally described as 'foxy', and the full red wines made from grapes such as Concord and Isabella taste strongly foxy, although the flavour is less noticeable in 'sherries' and in sparkling wines. Good 'champagne' is made both by the *méthode champenoise* and by tank fermentation using Catawba and Delaware grapes. More recently, experiments have been conducted to acclimatize European vines such as Chardonnay, Riesling and Pinot Noir in the east, and these seem to be achieving quite some success.

Prohibition was a severe blow to commercial wine growing in the USA, though it has been estimated that 1,600,000 hl (35 million gallons) of home-made wines were produced during that period. The recovery, particularly in the post-war period, has been remarkable, and many Californian growers have responded with great energy to the new preference for lighter table wines as opposed to the full-bodied sweeter wines that have long been produced in great quantity. One of the most significant developments is the trend away from borrowed European names towards naming the wine from the grape it is made from. It is now a legal requirement that at least 51% of the wine should be from that grape and the rest from grapes that blend well with it, and that all the wine must come from the area designated on the label. American wine labels now show a justified pride in a fine product, which has no need to masquerade under borrowed names.

Mechanical cultivation in California

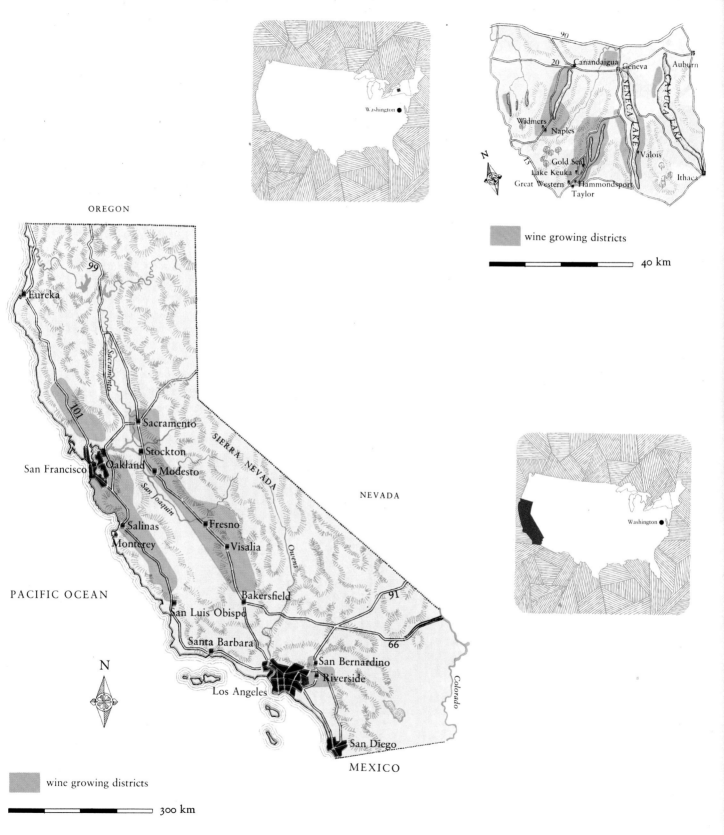

OREGON

99

Eureka

Sacramento

101

San Francisco
Oakland
Sacramento
Stockton
Modesto
San Joaquin

SIERRA NEVADA

Salinas
Monterey
Fresno
Visalia

NEVADA

Owens

PACIFIC OCEAN

Bakersfield

91

San Luis Obispo

66

Santa Barbara

San Bernardino
Riverside

Colorado

N

Los Angeles

San Diego

MEXICO

wine growing districts

300 km

90

Canandaigua
Geneva
Auburn

20

SENECA LAKE

CAYUGA LAKE

Widmers
Naples

Valois

15

Gold Seal
Lake Keuka

Great Western
Hammondsport
Taylor

Ithaca

N

wine growing districts

40 km

Washington

Washington

149

Napa Valley

The Napa Valley, lying to the north of San Francisco, produces some of the finest Californian wines. South of the city is the Salinas Valley, an area of considerable expansion at the present time, where excellent wines are grown, and inland is the Central Valley, where the mass-produced 'port' and 'sherry' and local specialities such as the sweet Angelica are made. However, even here refrigeration is making possible the manufacture of good table wines.

The exploitation of the Napa Valley for wine-growing dates from the planting in 1857 of the Buena Vista vineyards by the Hungarian Colonel Agoston Haraszthy. These are at Sonoma, strictly speaking in a neighbouring and rival area to Napa. Haraszthy brought many vines from Europe, including probably the Hungarian Zinfandel grape, from which one of the most individual Californian wines (comparable to a Beaujolais) is still made at Buena Vista. All the grapes grown in California are of European origin, but the wine gains its local character from the climate and the soil. The white wines are made largely from the Chardonnay and the Johannisberg Riesling, the best reds from the Cabernet Sauvignon and the Pinot Noir, and the rosés from the Grenache. A fruity red wine is also made from the Beaujolais Gamay, or Gamay Noir, and a strong full-bodied Barbera is a characteristic product of the Sebastiani winery. In the north of the valley sparkling wine is produced by the *méthode champenoise* at the Schramsberg Champagne Cellars.

Wine labels with these names or with names of Louis M. Martini, Beaulieu Vineyards, Inglenook or Charles Krug are a guarantee of well-made and individual Californian wine.

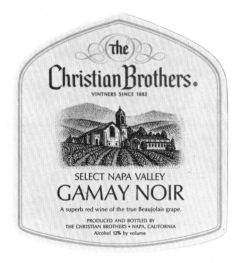

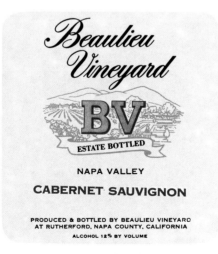

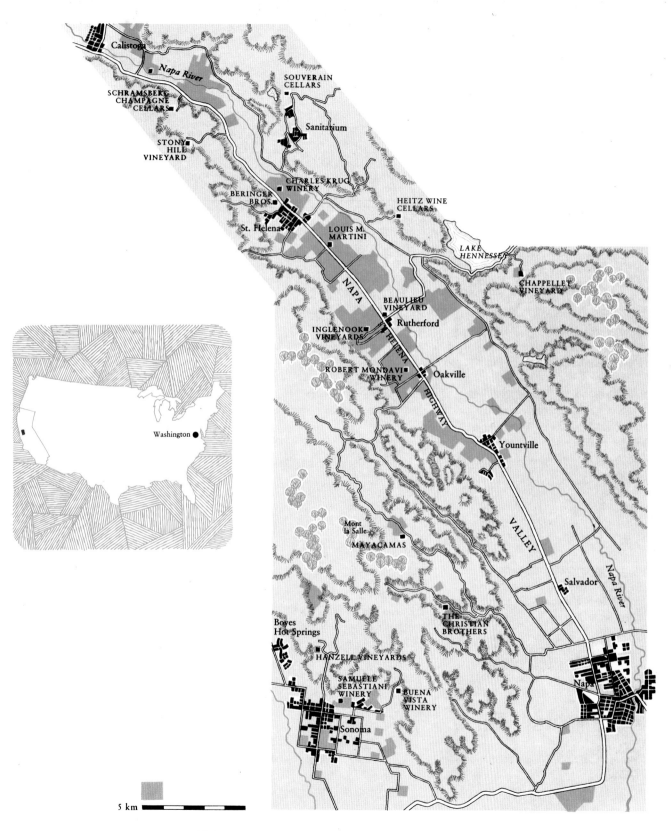

Calistoga

Napa River

SOUVERAIN
CELLARS

SCHRAMSBERG
CHAMPAGNE
CELLARS

Sanitarium

STONY
HILL
VINEYARD

CHARLES KRUG
WINERY

BERINGER
BROS.

HEITZ WINE
CELLARS

St. Helena

LOUIS M.
MARTINI

*LAKE
HENNESSEY*

CHAPPELLET
VINEYARD

BEAULIEU
VINEYARD

Rutherford

INGLENOOK
VINEYARDS

ROBERT MONDAVI
WINERY

Oakville

Yountville

Washington

Napa River

Mont
la Salle

MAYACAMAS

VALLEY

Salvador

Boyes
Hot Springs

THE
CHRISTIAN
BROTHERS

HANZELL VINEYARDS

Napa

SAMUELE
SEBASTIANI
WINERY

BUENA
VISTA
WINERY

Sonoma

5 km

South America

The middle regions of South America – the south of Brazil, Uruguay, Argentina and Chile – account for a tenth of the world's total wine production. Argentina produces the greater part of this, but most of it is absorbed by the home market. Most Argentine wines are comparable to cheap Spanish types.

Brazil and Uruguay make wines of rather dubious quality, from a variety of hybrids of American and European vines. By far the best South American wines come from Chile, from the area around Santiago where the climate is well suited to viticulture. German immigrants in particular have achieved a great deal here.

Many European vines have been planted in Chile, including Cabernet Sauvignon, Riesling, Pinot Noir and Pinot Gris. Red wines from Bordeaux

major wine districts

lesser wine districts

1000 km

Vineyards in Argentina

vines are good; dry, light and fruity, they age extremely well and attain balance and elegance.

The red wines from the Pinot Noir have a pleasant, spicy roundness. The Riesling is the best of the white varieties.

Wine growing in Chile is still in process of development and it looks as if it will become the most important wineland of the New World.

Unfortunately the Chileans too are rather careless about nomenclature. 'Rheinwein' or 'Chilean Burgundy' is cheerfully printed on labels, but changes are beginning to be made. Designations like 'Tipo Chablis' and 'Tipo Borgoña' (Chablis type, Burgundy type) are increasingly used. Good quality wines are usually labelled with a brand name and their place of origin. Just occasionally Chilean wine is encountered in Europe.

Wine bottles

The bottle and the cork were brought together in the seventeenth century and since that time it has been possible to age wine in the bottle. The various wine-growing regions have their own traditional types of bottle.

1 Sherry bottles are mostly conventional in shape with a fairly long neck.
2 Tapering bottles are used for Loire wines.
3 A champagne bottle has to withstand a good deal of pressure and it is therefore heavy, thick and sturdy, with an indentation in which you put your thumb when pouring. Champagne bottles are always done up in festive gold or silver paper.
4 The classical Bordeaux bottle with a long neck and clearly defined shoulders.
5 Broad bottle with sloping shoulders for Burgundy and Beaujolais.
6 Alsace wines come in tall, slender green bottles.
7 Slender bottles are also used for Rhine and Moselle wines – brown for Rhine wines, green for Moselle.
8 The familiar straw-jacketed Chianti bottle which dates from a time when glass was expensive and worth protecting in this way, and handwork was cheap. The straw coverings are still woven by women, particularly around Poggibonsi in the Chianti district.
9 The Beaujolais 'pot', inspired by the old hand-blown bottles.
10 Graceful bottle inspired by the Greek amphora, used for Côtes de Provence wines.

Uncorking

Remove the foil only as far as the rim of the bottle. Use a good corkscrew, one with its thread properly centred and true; if you use a poor corkscrew you are always liable to crumble the cork. Pull the cork carefully and without letting it pop, and wipe the neck of the bottle clean with a napkin.

Champagne

Untwist the wires. The cork hardly ever flies out. It usually has to be eased out under a napkin – the latter also serves to smother the popping sound. Be particularly careful when uncorking champagne not to break the cork.

Official classifications of French wines

Les grands vins de Bordeaux

name of growth	commune
PREMIERS GRANDS CRUS	
Château Lafite-Rothschild	Pauillac
Château Latour	Pauillac
Château Margaux	Margaux
Château Haut-Brion	Pessac (Graves!)
Château Mouton-Rothschild	Pauillac
DEUXIÈMES GRANDS CRUS	
Château Rausan-Ségla	Margaux
Château Rauzan-Gassies	Margaux
Château Léoville-Lascases	St-Julien
Château Léoville-Poyferré	St-Julien
Château Léoville-Barton	St-Julien
Château Durfort-Vivens	Margaux
Château Lascombes	Margaux
Château Gruaud-Larose	St-Julien
Château Brane-Cantenac	Cantenac
Château Pichon-Longueville	Pauillac
Château Pichon-Longueville-Comtesse de Lalande	Pauillac
Château Ducru-Beaucaillou	St-Julien
Château Cos-d'Estournel	St-Estèphe
Château Montrose	St-Estèphe
TROISIÈMES GRANDS CRUS	
Château Kirwan	Cantenac
Château d'Issan	Cantenac
Château Lagrange	St-Julien
Château Langoa	St-Julien
Château Palmer	Cantenac
Château Cantenac-Brown	Cantenac
Château Giscours	Labarde
Château Malescot-St-Exupéry	Margaux
Château Desmirail	Margaux
Château Marquis d'Alesme-Becker	Margaux

name of growth	commune
Château Ferrière	Margaux
Château La Lagune	Ludon
Château Calon-Ségur	St-Estèphe
Château Boyd-Cantenac	Cantenac
QUATRIÈMES GRANDS CRUS	
Château St-Pierre-Sevaistre	St-Julien
Château St-Pierre-Bontemps	St-Julien
Château Branaire-Ducru	St-Julien
Château Talbot	St-Julien
Château Duhart-Milon	Pauillac
Château Beychevelle	St-Julien
Château Pouget	Cantenac
Château La Tour-Carnet	St-Laurent
Château Lafon-Rochet	St-Estèphe
Château Le Prieuré-Lichine	Cantenac
Château Marquis de Terme	Margaux
CINQUIÈMES GRANDS CRUS	
Château Pontet-Canet	Pauillac
Château Batailley	Pauillac
Château Haut-Batailley	Pauillac
Château Grand-Puy-Lacoste	Pauillac
Château Grand-Puy-Ducasse	Pauillac
Château Lynch-Bages	Pauillac
Château Lynch-Moussas	Pauillac
Château Mouton-Baron Philippe	Pauillac
Château Croizet-Bages	Pauillac
Château Haut-Bages-Libéral	Pauillac
Château Pédesclaux	Pauillac
Château Clerc-Milon-Mondon	Pauillac
Château Dauzac	Labarde
Château du Tertre	Arsac
Château Belgrave	St-Laurent
Château Camensac	St-Laurent
Château Cos-Labory	St-Estèphe
Château Cantemerle	Macau

Les grands vins blancs de Sauternes

name of growth	commune
PREMIER GRAND CRU	
Château d'Yquem (Marquis de Lur-Saluces)	Sauternes
PREMIERS CRUS	
Château Guiraud	Sauternes
Château La Tour Blanche	Bommes
Château de Rayne-Vigneau	Bommes
Château Rabaud-Promis	Bommes
Château Sigalas-Rabaud	Bommes
Château Lafaurie-Peyraguey	Bommes
Clos Haut-Peyraguey	Bommes
Château Coutet	Barsac
Château Climens	Barsac
Château Suduiraut	Preignac
Château Rieussec	Fargues
DEUXIÈMES CRUS	
Château d'Arche	Sauternes
Château d'Arche-Lafaurie	Sauternes
Château Filhot	Sauternes
Château Lamothe	Sauternes
Château Lamothe-Bergey	Sauternes
Château Myrat	Barsac
Château Doisy-Daëne	Barsac
Château Doisy-Védrines	Barsac
Château Doisy-Dubroca	Barsac
Château Suau	Barsac
Château Broustet	Barsac
Château Nairac	Barsac
Château Caillou	Barsac
Château de Malle	Preignac
Château Romer	Fargues

St-Emilion

Grands crus de Pomerol

Les grands vins blancs de la Côte d'Or

Les grands vins rouges de la Côte d'Or

vineyard	commune	vineyard	commune
		Les Corvées	Prémeaux
		Les Didiers	Prémeaux
PREMIERS CRUS		Les Forêts	Prémeaux
Le St-Georges	Nuits-St-Georges	Santenots du Milieu	Meursault
Aux Murgers	Nuits-St-George	Clos-des-Mouches	Beaune
Les Cailles	Nuits-St-George	Les Marconnets	Beaune
Porrets	Nuits-St-George	Les Grèves	Beaune
Pruliers	Nuits-St-George	Les Fèves	Beaune
Les Vaucrains	Nuits-St-George	La Boudriotte	Chassagne
Les Beaux Monts	Vosne-Romanée	Clos St-Jean	Chassagne
Les Malconsorts	Vosne-Romanée	Les Epenots	Pommard
Les Angles	Volnay	Les Rugiens-Bas	Pommard
La Barre	Volnay	Les Gravières	Santenay
Bousse d'Or	Volnay	Les Hauts-Jarrons	Savigny-les-Beaune
Caillerets	Volnay		
Champans	Volnay		

Vintage chart for French wines

year	red Bordeaux	white Bordeaux	red Burgundy	white Burgundy	Côtes-du-Rhône	Alsace	Pouilly-sur-Loire Sancerre	Anjou Touraine	Champagne
1950	***	**		***	***			**	
1952	**	***	***	***	****	no longer available	no longer available	**	Best years: these vary with the brands; but the years 1961, 1964 and 1966 are particularly recommended
1953	****	***	***	***	**			***	
1955	*****	****	***	***	***			***	
1957	**	***	**	***	***			***	
1959	***	****	****	***	**			***	
1961	*****	****	****	***	****			***	
1962	****	****	***	***	***			***	
1964	***	***	****	***	***	***	***	***	
1966	****	****	****	***	***	****	***	***	
1967	***	***	***	***	***	***	**	**	
1969	**	**	****	****	*	****	***	***	
1970	****	****	**	***	***	***	***	***	
1971	***	***	***	***	***	*****	***	***	

* moderate year   ** fair to good   *** good   **** very good   ***** a great year

German Wine Laws

Wine and Food

New German legislation came into force in 1971. Its main purpose was clarification and more careful definition of the nomenclature and descriptions of quality used on German wine labels. The latter were to be a more reliable guide to, and guarantee of, the contents than had hitherto been the case. Since under the new legislation all *Qualitätsweine* have to be *naturrein* (pure), that is to say without the addition of sugar or other substances, this and other similar descriptions no longer appear on labels. The place of origin of the wine is now more strictly defined. Districts or sites may only be named on the label if the wine has actually been grown there: wines can no longer 'borrow' a well-known site name in their vicinity.

CATEGORIES

1 *(Deutscher) Tafelwein* German table wine
2 *Qualitätswein* superior wine, from a specified district: these, in their German forms, are Ahr, Hessische Bergstrasse, Mittelrhein, Mosel-Saar-Ruwer, Nahe, Rheingau, Rheinhessen, Rheinpfalz, Franken, Württemberg, Baden
3 *Qualitätswein mit Prädikat* superior wine from a specified district, with an additional description of quality. The prescribed terms are:
Kabinett: special reserve
Spätlese: late-picked, fully ripe grapes
Auslese: selected fully ripe bunches
Beerenauslese: selected fully ripe grapes
Trockenbeerenauslese: selected overripe grapes, shrivelled and affected by the 'noble rot' *(Botrytis cinerea)*

Eiswein, 'ice wine', is an extra specification added to the above descriptions when the grapes have been picked with the frost still on them and the juice frozen.

APÉRITIFS	dry sherry, dry Madeira, vermouth, dry champagne or a light, dry white wine (such as Alsace or Loire wines) or a dry rosé (Tavel)
STARTERS AND HORS D'OEUVRES	
oysters	dry champagne, Chablis, Alsace Riesling, Muscadet
smoked salmon	Alsace Riesling, dry Rhine wine
ham	Alsace Riesling, white Burgundy, Moselle
pâté	dry white Bordeaux, Alsace, Tokay, white Loire wine, dry Madeira
mixed hors d'oeuvres	Moselle, dry champagne, Alsace wines
SOUP	sherry or Madeira
FISH	
fried	dry white Bordeaux, white Burgundy, Alsace Tokay, Rhine wine, Loire wine
in a creamy sauce	white Burgundy, dry or semi-sec white Bordeaux, Loire wine, Alsace wine
in a butter sauce	Alsace Riesling, Loire wines, Rhine wines, Moselle
mussels	Muscadet, Moselle
crab and other shellfish	dry champagne, Muscadet, dry white Bordeaux, white Burgundy
WHITE MEAT AND CHICKEN	light red wines (Beaujolais, Bordeaux) also Alsace Riesling, Rhine wine
PORK	Alsace wine, Rhine wine, Moselle
RED MEAT	practically all red wines: Beaujolais, Burgundy, Bordeaux, Rhône wines, red Loire wines, Rioja
GAME	heavy red wines: St-Emilion, Rhône wines, Burgundy
MEAT IN PIQUANT SAUCES	Rhône wines, Corbières, Côtes de Provence, Rioja
MEAT FONDUE	Beaujolais, Rhône wines, Côtes de Provence, Corbières, Rioja, Chianti
CHEESE	
soft cream cheeses, goat cheeses	white wines
Stilton, mild Cheddar, Dutch cheese	port, red Burgundy, Bordeaux
piquant French cheeses	young, strong wines: Beaujolais, Rhône wines, Rioja, Corbières, Côtes de Provence
Italian cheese	Chianti, Valpolicella
Swiss cheese	Swiss and other white wines, red wine
SWEET DISHES AND DESSERT	
tarts, flans, pastries, crêpes	sweet white wines (Sauternes, Monbazillac), cream sherry, sweet champagne
FRUIT	sweet white wines (Sauternes, Monbazillac), port, Madeira